THE MORALITY OF CONSENT

THE MORALITY
OF CONSENT

Alexander M. Bickel

New Haven and London   Yale University Press

1975

Originally published with assistance from the Louis Effingham DeForest Memorial Fund.

Library of Congress catalog card number: 75–10988
International standard book number: 0–300–01911–4

Designed by John O. C. McCrillis
and set in Times Roman type.

Printed in the United States of America by
The Alpine Press, South Braintree, Mass.

Published in Great Britain, Europe, and Africa by
Yale University Press, Ltd., London.

Distributed in Latin America by Kaiman & Polon,
Inc., New York City; in Australasia by Book & Film
Services, Artarmon, N.S.W., Australia; in India by
UBS Publishers' Distributors Pvt. Ltd., Delhi;
in Japan by John Weatherhill, Inc., Tokyo.

The following articles, which appear in this book, are used here with permission:

"The Aims of Education and the Proper Standards of the University," reprinted from *Minerva* 12, number 2 (April 1974), 199–206.

"Press and Government: Aspects of the Constitutional Position," delivered at the Freedom House Consultation, "The News Media and the Government: Clash of Concentrated Power," 26 June 1973; published in *Freedom at Issue,* September–October 1973.

"Citizenship in the American Constitution," *Arizona Law Review* 15 (1973), 369–87. Copyright © 1975 by the Arizona Board of Regents. Reprinted by permission.

"Dissenting and Concurring Opinions I," *The Public Interest,* number 22 (Winter 1971), 25–28. Copyright © 1971 by National Affairs, Inc.

"The Game Rules of a Free Press," reprinted in *Congress Bi-Weekly,* 9 March 1973 from a paper prepared for an American Jewish Congress Conference on Government and the Media.

Contents

Acknowledgments

Alexander M. Bickel died on November 7, 1974. At his death he had left the manuscript for this book, which is based on his William C. DeVane lectures delivered at Yale University. The manuscript was prepared for publication by Jeannette Hopkins.

Several of the lectures had been revised by the author for publication in journals. Chapter 1, section 2, appeared in substantially the same form in the *New Republic*, 17 March 1973. Part of chapter 2 appeared in somewhat different form in the *Arizona Law Review* 15, 1973. Part of chapter 3 appeared in somewhat different form in *Commentary*, November 1972, and part of chapter 4 also was printed in *Commentary*, January 1974. Part of chapter 5 appeared in *Minerva* 12, number 2 (April 1974). Brief passages from this book appeared also in *Commentary*, January 1971 and July 1972; *New Republic*, 12 July 1969, 13 June 1970, 17 October 1970, and 28 October 1972; *Freedom at Issue*, September-October 1973; *The Public Interest*, number 22 (Winter 1971); and *Congress Bi-Weekly,* volume 40, number 5, (March 1973).

The bibliography is a composite of one which appeared in the *Yale Law Journal* (84 Yale L. J. 201–04, 1974) and one prepared by Solomon C. Smith, reference librarian of the Yale Law Library.

The footnotes were prepared with the assistance of Dwight Monson and Lynne Johnson. Mrs. Isabel Poludnewycz typed the manuscript, and the index was prepared by Meira Pimsleur.

1

Constitutionalism and the Political Process

1

Constitutionalism and the Political Process

Political Thought and Democratic Process

Two diverging traditions in the mainstream of Western political thought—one "liberal," the other "conservative"—have competed, and still compete, for control of the democratic process and of the American constitutional system; both have controlled the direction of our judicial policy at one time or another.

One of these, the contractarian tradition, began with the moderate common sense of John Locke. It was pursued by Rousseau, and it long ago captured, and substantially retains possession of, the label liberal, although I would contest its title to it. The other tradition can, for lack of a better term, be called Whig in the English eighteenth-century sense. It is usually called conservative, and I would associate it chiefly with Edmund Burke. This is my own model.

These two traditions—contractarian and Whig—converge in their attitudes toward revolutionary activity. Both, for example, are hostile to any civil disobedience, designed to redress grievances, that is premised on the iniquity or inutility of the political system—that attacks the entire system rather than flaws within it. But except for this significant but delusive convergence, the two traditions tend to go separate ways; they diverged in response to the impact of the French Revolution on political thought.

The liberal contractarian model rests on a vision of individual rights that have a clearly defined, independent existence predating society and are derived from nature and from a natural, if imagined, contract. Society must bend to these rights. As John Rawls, the most recent philosopher of this tradition, says, these rights are lexically prior.[1] They condition everything, and society operates within limits they set. Deduced from premises that cannot be questioned closely, they must themselves be deduced by pure reason.

The Whig model, on the other hand, begins not with theoretical rights but with a real society, whose origins in the historical mists it acknowledges to be mysterious. The Whig model assesses human nature as it is seen to be. It judges how readily and how far men can be moved by means other than violent, that is to say, how far they can be moved by government. The values of such a society evolve, but as of any particular moment they are taken as given. Limits are set by culture, by time- and place-bound conditions, and within these limits the task of government informed by the present state of values is to make a peaceable, good, and improving society. That, and not anything that existed prior to society itself and that now exists independently of society, is what men have a right to. The Whig model obviously is flexible, pragmatic, slow-moving, highly political. It partakes, in substantial measure, of the relativism that pervades Justice Oliver Wendell Holmes's theory of the First Amendment,[2] although not to its ultimate logical exaggeration. Lacking a catechism of shared values, such as religious societies may cherish, it has no choice but relativism. The alternative is the tyranny of some of us over the others. Without carrying matters to a logical extreme, indeed without pretense to intellectual valor, and without sanguine spirit, the Whig model rests on a mature skepticism. It places enormous reliance on the political marketplace, which may in some measure be, as Holmes was pleased to say, a marketplace of ideas, but

1. John Rawls, *A Theory of Justice* (Cambridge: Harvard University Press, Belknap Press, 1971).
2. See Schenck v. United States, 249 U.S. 47 (1919).

one where ideas and the vote are not the only bargaining units. It is a market that is in continuous, not only quadrennial or biennial, session. As was true even for Holmes, the Whig system is not altogether value-free. The unexamined life, said Socrates, is not worth living. Nor is it bearable. To acknowledge no values at all is to deny a difference between ourselves and other particles that tumble in space. The irreducible value, though not the exclusive one, is the idea of law. Law is more than just another opinion; not because it embodies all right values, or because the values it does embody tend from time to time to reflect those of a majority or plurality, but because it is the value of values. Law is the principal institution through which a society can assert its values.

The contractarian model, in contrast, is committed not to law alone but to a parochial faith in a closely calibrated scale of values. It is moral, principled, legalistic, ultimately authoritarian. It is weak on pragmatism, strong on theory. For it, law is not so much a process, and certainly not a process in continual flux, as it is a body of rules binding all, rules that can be changed only by the same formal method by which they were enacted. The relationship between the individual and government is defined by law; as are the entire public life of the society and, indeed, the society itself. Law has its origins in a contract, an imagined legal transaction. The concept of citizenship is, therefore, central, defining the parties to the original contract and the membership of the society.

This concept of contract was central to Chief Justice Roger Brooke Taney, who wrote the decision of the Supreme Court in the *Dred Scott* case[3] and who was a liberal. It was central to the Earl Warren Court, which used virtually the same language Taney had used. The repetition was unwitting, but not accidental. For in the contractarian model, citizenship is *the* relationship between some individuals and the state. The United States would correspond much more closely to the contractarian model today if its constitutional development had taken place under the privileges and immunities of citizens clause of section 1 of the Four-

3. Scott v. Sandford, 60 U.S. (19 Howard) 393 (1857).

teenth Amendment, instead of, as it did, under the due process and equal protection clauses. There would have been a more theoretical evolution of abstract rights, tending to the absolute and presumed to have an independent prior existence, rather than the pragmatic development that did occur. Words and concepts, such as those of due process and equal protection, are only words and concepts, to be sure, but they breed attitudes, they tend toward a mind-set, they influence future thought and action.

In the political process, majoritarianism is everything for the liberal contractarian. The vote is all important, the franchise must be universally available, absolute equality of the vote and equality of the size of constituencies are essential. Speech must be wholly untrammelled for it is the engine of the majoritarian political process. A bright line is drawn between speech and conduct, because conduct is not politically significant. It has no part in the formation of law, which is entirely legislative and litigious and depends on speech alone. It is also no accident, then, that the Warren Court loosened those procedural and jurisdictional rules which require concreteness, actuality, and immediacy in the clash between state law and a supposed higher federal law, before permitting litigation of the validity of state law itself. In the political process of self-help that violates the local law in order to invoke the higher authority (a process invited by the rules that were relaxed by the Warren Court), conduct rather than mere speech is critical. The Warren Court permitted litigation at earlier stages, thus disinviting what the rules have a tendency to invite, disobedience of local law.[4] Do not engage in self-help, the Warren Court was saying: litigate at the earliest possible opportunity. And, otherwise, vote.

Majoritarianism, like the market theory of the First Amendment, presents a dilemma and a paradox in contractarian thought.

---

4. Chief Justice Earl Warren showed a rare awareness of the import of these rules in a dissent in a case where the point was in fact irrelevant. The rules have required, he noted, "that persons seeking to challenge the constitutionality of a statute first violate it to establish their standing to sue." Walker v. Birmingham, 388 U.S. 307, 327. But the insight was fleeting. The chief justice did not elsewhere draw the consequences from it.

To use the economist's term, it presents a problem of market definition. A realistic majoritarianism makes sense only in the smallest kind of city-state constituency. The town meeting is the paradigm. James Madison thought that, in a small constituency, real and coherent and continuous majorities are possible, and that they are dangerous because they are likely to tyrannize the minority. For this reason he thought well of the Union, which enlarged the American constituencies to national size, thus making majorities less coherent. For contractarian theory, this enlargement of the constituency is necessary if reliance is to be placed on majoritarian decisions. After all, what kind of a market place of ideas is it if it is restricted to a town meeting in Hamden, Connecticut? Such a small marketplace is unlikely to ventilate all ideas and to make a choice that deserves to be relied on as true or valuable, or that deserves to be enforced. The truth that a handful of people find in their own small marketplace may be their truth; a claim of universal validity for it will be difficult to make, however. And as the constituency is enlarged, majoritarianism steadily loses all reality as a policy-making mechanism. It becomes, as Madison foresaw, one mechanism in the complex system Professor Robert Dahl has described as rule by collections of minorities from time to time.

The First Amendment presents a similar dilemma. As audiences grow into mass audiences, it is more and more difficult to assume that they can be reasoned with, and to assume that in the marketplace of ideas truth will drive out error and good counsels prevail over bad. It is the paradox of liberal contractarian moralism that society must bend to a catechism of principles, hence a moralism not a little infected with authoritarianism. Yet among its principles are egalitarianism, popular sovereignty, and free speech, which can produce outcomes contrary to the authoritarianism the catechism implies. Rousseau resolved this paradox by resort to the notion of a general will, a fundamentally anti-democratic notion. Even so, the approving, indeed enchanted, historian of the Enlightenment, Peter Gay, must allow that Rousseau's ideas, while fine as criticism, "are at best unrealistic and at worst pernicious" as a constructive program. Rousseau, Professor Gay continues, "tells us that freedom and equality, far from being incompatible, are indispensable to each other; that the political public must be absolutely general; and that institutional forms are less important than the moral and social foundations of citizenship. But Rousseau is not the philosopher of the democratic state, which rests on the very tensions that Rousseau wants to abolish."[5]

When the aims of the democratic movement, as Rousseau conceived them, conflicted with majoritarianism and the democratic state, Rousseau escaped, or at least his followers did, into authoritarianism and the antidemocratic state. In our system the liberal contractarian finds his escape in the Constitution, which, speaking through the Supreme Court, limits majority rule. The liberal contractarian sought to end the Vietnam war by urging that the Court declare the war itself unconstitutional. This effort failed not because the war was not unconstitutional—in my view, President Johnson did exceed his constitutional authority in extending the war—but because, as a practical matter, resort to political rather than judicial government seemed the better remedy. The political decision to commit the nation to full-scale war was rejected politically, and the consequence was a strengthening of the process of consent.

In the liberal contractarian view, the limits on majority rule through appeal to the Constitution tend to be absolute, timeless, in response to the resistance of a majority, or even a minority. Most of life is seen in moral rather than prudential terms. None of the pragmatic skepticism so salient in the Whig model infects the Constitution of the contractarian. This was Justice Hugo Black's Constitution, a storehouse of principles, inflexible and numerous. Hugo Black was himself a man of fiercely held principles. He believed in law—pervasive, positive, virtually all-encompassing law—which secured and defined the rights of the citizen and enclosed and regulated his life. He could find no right of privacy in the Constitution at all, and, perfectly consistently, could not accommodate himself or his legal universe to extralegal political and social action. His vision was of a legalitarian society.

5. Peter Gay, *The Party of Humanity* (paper ed., 1971), pp. 259–60.

He was a judicial activist, quick to regulate what seemed disordered and unruly. He was indeed an imperialist of law, judicial and majoritarian law both, for like Taney, he was also a populist who resolved the tension between legalitarianism and populism by force of will. Black was in everything but blood, and for all we know in that, too, a direct lineal descendant of Andrew Jackson, another populist and a great majoritarian democratizer, but who wrote in a letter in 1821: "I have an opinion of my own on all subjects, and when that opinion is formed I pursue it *publickly* regardless of who goes with me." Black could have said as much. Nothing is easier for strong-minded, passionate men, the true believers, who are given, in a phrase of Richard Hofstadter, to "self-assertive subjectivism"—nothing is easier for such men than to attribute their passionate beliefs to a monolithic abstraction called the people or the Constitution. The Warren Court in its heyday was Hugo Black writ large.

Justice Black's opinions in demonstration cases are characteristic of his career.[6] The results he reached—with which I do not necessarily quarrel—led many of his admirers to conclude that he was aging and reverting atavistically to some earlier conservative strain in his makeup. This was entirely false. The opinions are a consistent and integral part of his conception of the legal order, and indeed serve to complete and explain it. They constitute a rather aggrieved lecture to the demonstrators. You have had, Black admonishes them in effect, a marvelously expansive, generous, good system of values which the Supreme Court has defined for you and has sustained by law. Now, after fifteen years of this kind of fulfillment, you resort not to law but to self-help, and you seem to express dissatisfaction with the lawgiver's values and seem inclined to generate some of your own. Well, the law must not and will not let you behave in this fashion, by these methods, in pursuit of such objectives.

The Court—Black was as often as not in dissent—in none of these cases laid down significant principles of civil disobedience,

6. See Cox v. Louisiana, 379 U.S. 559 (1965); Brown v. Louisiana, 383 U.S. 131 (1966).

or exhibited large permissive attitudes toward disruption. It was doing what it does best; it was seeking some procedural accommodation to avoid the clash of ultimates. But Black addressed ultimates here just as passionately as in his First Amendment opinions, invoking the shade of John Lillburn and defending an absolute right to self-expression and to conscience. He found a measure of ingratitude and incontinence on the part of those to whom beneficent law had been given and who would have none of it: "Those who encourage minority groups to believe" that they have a right to "patrol and picket in the streets whenever they choose in order to advance what they think to be a just and noble end, do no service to those minority groups. . . . The history of the past 25 years if it shows nothing else shows that [this] group's . . . rights have to be protected by the courts, which must be kept free from intimidation and coercive pressures of any kind."[7] Again: "It is an unhappy circumstance," he wrote, ". . . that the group, which more than any other has needed a government of equal laws and equal justice, is now encouraged to believe that the best way for it to advance its cause, which is a worthy one, is by taking the law into its own hands from place to place and from time to time." For this sort of self-help, "[g]overnments like ours were formed to substitute the rule of law."[8] Black is thus the representative figure of the liberal in American constitutionalism—a moralist who used the Constitution as a compendium of numerous, precisely framed, generally absolute principles to make a sort of peace—or truce, at least—with the majoritarian populist he also was.

Of course, nobody who wreaks himself upon the world, as Holmes used to say, in an active career of fifty years' duration leaves behind a wholly coherent and self-consistent philosophy of law and politics, or of the Constitution, or even of a single large subject of constitutional adjudication. Men like Black, or Holmes, or Louis D. Brandeis, or Felix Frankfurter, or Justices John Marshall, Roger B. Taney, Stephen J. Field, Samuel F. Miller,

7. Cox v. Louisiana, 379 U.S. at 584.
8. Brown v. Louisiana, 383 U.S. at 167–68.

or Joseph P. Bradley before them, were engaged in a life of doing, not of scholarly contemplation and system-building. Any attempt to draw from such lives a coherent, self-consistent view of the system that underlay the life work commits some injustice; it is never entirely possible to know what a person would have considered aberrational and inconsistent in his own thought, and what central and characteristic. But we infer what we can from the evidence taken as a whole from the work of such men. It is, as it must be, an exercise in judgment and is not infallible.

In our own time, loyalty to the liberal catechism has led to a traumatic conflict of principles that Burke could have anticipated. Vietnam was no conventional imperialist war. Wrong and morally wrong in its conduct and consequences, it was nevertheless not evil in intent or origin. What propelled us into this war was a corruption of the generous, idealistic, liberal impulse which, together with a sense of legitimate self-interest, informed and sustained America's foreign policy through the Second World War and in the years after. I use the word corruption to connote not evil but merely decay. Our self-interest began to be invoked mechanically rather than realistically, and the altruistic impulse decayed into self-assurance and self-righteousness; it became, as generosity and idealism assuredly can, oppressive, and in the end cruel. Liberal, generous ideology often decays in this fashion, as does religious ideology. Of course, such ideologies sometimes draw to themselves authoritarian and otherwise morally deficient personalities. But the seeds of decay are within the ideologies themselves, in their pretensions to universality, in their overconfident assaults on the variety and unruliness of the human condition, in the intellectual and emotional imperialism of concepts like freedom, equality, even peace.

Edmund Burke and Political Reason

In our time of dogma to the left and dogma to the right, of unvarnished populism to the left and to the right, when, in a phrase of Burke, "rival follies" mutually wage an unrelenting war and when change is widely counted a self-evident virtue, there is much to learn from Burke, the seminal, if not the representative figure of the Whig tradition. Our problem is the totalitarian tendency of the democratic faith, and the apparent inconsistency of most remedies for that condition. Our problem has been, and is most acutely now, the tyrannical tendency of ideas and the suicidal emptiness of a politics without ideas, "the opposite evils," in another phrase of Burke, "of intolerance and of indifference."

"Who now reads Bolingbroke? Who ever read him through?" asked Burke in 1790 in the *Reflections*. And who now reads Burke? Though always brilliantly quotable, the prose is unfashionable and there is too much of it. It takes a lot of digging to get to the quotations. As for the substance, Burke speaks for the side that lost, resoundingly, quite a while ago. "When our grandchildren have made up their minds, once for all," wrote John Morley in 1888, "as to the merits of the social transformation which dawned on Europe in 1789, then Burke's *Reflections* will become a mere literary antiquity, and not before."[9] Morley's grandchildren, if not his children, did make up their minds, and his great-great-grandchildren do not remember what the problem was that called for the making up of minds.

But there was a problem. Enormous, in our eyes incredible, social injustices have been gradually remedied in the nearly two centuries since the French Revolution, although others remain or have newly appeared. Perhaps the good that has been achieved is a legacy of the revolution, and perhaps it is not. But this is certain: the French Revolution was the first of the totalitarian movements to drench the Western world in blood, particularly in our own century. This is what Burke prophetically saw and hated.

"Is it an infirmity to wish," asked Morley, that some "phrase of generous hope," such as "lighted up in the spirits" of Wordsworth, of Coleridge, and of Charles James Fox, "had escaped from Burke" on the fall of the Bastille?[10] The large-hearted Fox

9. John Morley, *Burke* (London and New York: Macmillan and Co., 1879), p. 210.
10. Ibid., p. 211.

exclaimed: "How much the greatest event it is that ever happened in the world, and how much the best."[11] It was a fatuous remark, like Lincoln Steffens' when he came back from the Soviet Union thinking he had been into the future and seen it work, or like many a now charitably forgotten celebration of one or another wave of the future in the 1930s. And it is an infirmity to wish that Burke had said something of the sort. For it would have been the expression at best of a "fine illusion," as Morley himself implies, and not necessarily fine at that.

Burke saw further and deeper instantly and without illusion. He saw a "chaos of levity and ferocity." He was no more given to automatic adulation of "the people" than of kings, knowing that "liberty, when men act in bodies, is *power*," and that power is to be judged by the use that is made of it, by its distribution, and by the limits put on it. Simply the seizure of power by a great many enthusiastic people is in itself no cause for rejoicing. Burke knew that to begin by despising everything is to set up "trade without a capital," and he saw that the French revolutionaries, despising all about them, all their predecessors and all their contemporaries, must also "despise themselves until the moment in which they become truly despicable." Their liberty was not liberal, he wrote, their humanity was "savage and brutal." It was clear to him that moderation and reason—the very reason in whose name the revolution was made—would count for nothing in an escalation of fervor from one assembly to the next, until a soldier who could secure the obedience of the armies to himself "on his personal account" would become "the master of your Assembly, the master of your whole republic." Thus in 1790 did Burke unhesitatingly foretell the rise of Napoleon.

Then and for some years more, Burke beheld in England the spectacle of well-born, high-living swells—Fox's companions, despite all Fox's virtues and talents—and of high-minded dissenting divines, seeing only what they wanted to see and extolling the Parisian mobs ("excuse the term, it is still in use here," Burke

11. Quoted in Sir Philip Magnus, *Edmund Burke* (London: J. Murray, 1939), p. 185.

remarked) from Brooks' or from their pulpits. The French, these
safely distanced people were pleased to believe, had merely and
at long last acted on the principles of the English Revolution of
1688 and emulated the recent American one. Revolutionary
principles were all one, all equal, all good. They had, in fact,
too long been neglected in England itself. For the flaws of English
government were also gross. The rhetoric of these people was
ever apocalyptic. All that was wrong was wrong at the root and
all remedies had to be applied at the root. "Something they must
destroy," said Burke, "or they seem to themselves to exist for no
purpose." Mere reform would not do.

Burke understood his radical compatriots. He did not delude
himself about their steadiness of purpose. "Almost all the high-
bred republicans of my time have, after a short space," he
observed,

> become the most decided, thorough-paced courtiers; they
> soon left the business of a tedious, moderate, but practical
> resistance to those of us whom, in the pride and intoxication
> of their theories, they have slighted as not much better than
> Tories. . . . These professors, finding their extreme principles
> not applicable to cases which call only for a qualified or, as I
> may say, civil and legal resistance, in such cases employ no
> resistance at all. It is with them a war or a revolution, or it
> is nothing.

These men were not serious, but the revolution was, and they are
also to the extent that they are the ancestors of many a modern
contractarian liberal.

Though not often amused, Burke could sometimes dwell on
the radical chic hilarity of it all. "Is it not a singular phenome-
non," he wrote in a public letter to the Duke of Bedford, after
the *Reflections*, "that whilst the *sans-culotte* carcase-butchers,
and the philosophers of the shambles are pricking their dotted
lines upon his hide, and like the print of the poor ox that we see
at the shop-windows at Charing-cross, alive as he is, and thinking
no harm in the world, he is divided into rumps, and sirloins, and

briskets, and into all sort of pieces for roasting, boiling, and stewing, that wielders doing the bad and the unwise thing may be minimized, and so that when they do it anyway, the harm they cause will be less than total. And power should seek to rest on consent so that its distribution and its exercise may be stable—stability being a prime value, both as an end and as a means"; as an end, because though truth may be preferable to peace, "as we have scarcely ever the same certainty in the one that we have in the other, I would, unless the truth were evident indeed, hold fast to peace"; and as a means, because stability is a source as well as a fruit of consent, making the beneficent exercise of power possible though by no means certain.

A representative, electorally responsible institution was critical, therefore, not merely as a sharer of power, but as a generator of consent. Yet it was not the sole generator of consent, nor did it need to be elected by universal suffrage or to mirror its constituents' desires with perfect fidelity in order to be effective. Actually a parliament that is a creature strictly of a majority of the people "told by the head" was in Burke's view a menace, because it was all too likely to regard itself as sovereign, and to seize total power, riding roughshod over other institutions.

But it is necessary here to emphasize Burke's pragmatism and his sense of place and circumstance. Even though he saw clearly and in great detail what had gone wrong in France, he would not be drawn, in the course of controversies that raged following publication of the *Reflections*, into making affirmative recommendations for the structure and composition of French institutions. "I must see with my own eyes," he said,

> touch with my own hands, not only the fixed, but the momentary circumstances, before I would venture to suggest any political project whatsoever, I must know the power and disposition to accept, to execute, to persevere. . . . I must see the means of correcting the plan, where correctives would be wanted. I must see the things; I must see the men. . . . The eastern politicians never do anything without the opinion of the astrologers on the *fortunate moment*. . . .

Statesmen of a more judicious prescience look for the fortu-
nate moment too; but they seek it, not in the conjunctions
and oppositions of the planets, but in the conjunctions and
oppositions of men and things. These form their almanac.

In a system like the present one in the United States, therefore,
where the executive and a bicameral legislature have both evolved
toward election by universal suffrage, but from different constituencies and with staggered terms, Burke would not likely have
perceived the dangers that were so evident in the sovereign French
Assembly, and that might have arisen in eighteenth-century England from a sovereign House of Commons elected by universal
suffrage; although he would likely have diagnosed the same
danger in a Gaullist type of presidency, little countervailed by
parliamentary institutions and acting on the basis of the presumed
consent to its actions of the people, "told by the head" at the last
election of referendum. Even so, Burke wrote two years after the
Reflections that the English constitution was "not made for great,
general, and proscriptive exclusions [from the franchise, as of
Irish Catholics]; sooner or later it will destroy them, or they will
destroy the constitution."

The fundamental point was, and remains, that consent and
stability are not produced simply by the existence and function
of popularly elected institutions, although absolute power may be.
Elections, even if they are referenda, do not establish consent, or
do not establish it for long. They cannot mean that much. Masses
of people do not make clear-cut, long-range decisions. They do not
know enough about the issues, about themselves, their needs and
wishes, or about what those needs and wishes will appear to them
to be two months hence. "The will of the many and their interest
must very often differ"—an echo here, in some part, of Rousseau, but Burke did not suggest that anything positive followed
from this observation, such as the right of a minority, seized some-
how of the Rousseauian "general will," to rule. He argued only
that there was nothing natural or necessary about allowing a
majority to prevail. Rule by a majority obtained where it did, he
pointed out, by convention and habit, and did not obtain uni-

versally on all occasions and for all purposes even where established. And where a majority does rule unrestrained, it is capable of great and cruel oppression of minorities.

The people are something else than a majority registered on election day, although by convention and for lack of any other suitable method we let various majorities, including electoral ones, settle various things in various contexts on various occasions. The people begin with "the little platoon we belong to in society," what today we call groups, and they are found in places to which they are attached, in divisions of the country, what we call constituencies, which "have been formed by habit, and not by a sudden jerk of authority"—not by the assembly in Paris dividing France into equal squares, or by a reapportioning federal district judge, one might add, using a computer to so divide a state. No man will ever "glory in belonging to the Chequer No. 71," and yet "public affections," meaning consent to the institutions of government, must begin "in our families . . . pass on to our neighborhoods and our habitual provincial connexions," and so on to the nation. No jet age can change that.

The people then form into parties, under leadership they trust and find natural. Their temper, the temper of both the greater number and weight of them or of significant groups of them, is readily determinable, and no one can long govern against it, except by suppression, which is not government, as Burke remarked when urging conciliation with America. A nation, he said, "is not governed, which is perpetually to be conquered." Widespread dissatisfaction with government does not need the ballot box to express itself—Burke was far from deprecating direct political action, including civil disobedience in cases of necessity—and it must be met and conciliated, even if not shared by a numerical majority of the population, for law cannot deal with it. "I do not know the method," goes one of his most famous sentences, "of drawing up an indictment against an whole people."

The people, as Burke used the term, was a body in place, gathered, led, manifesting its temper in many ways and over a span of time as a whole, or as one or another sizable community within the whole body, not speaking merely on occasion in momentary numerical majorities. The influence of the people, so conceived, must be a dominant one because their consent is essential. That consent may be withdrawn regardless of elections; it must be preponderant, not merely majority consent, and is yielded not only and not even chiefly to the electoral verdict, but to institutions validated by time and familiarity and composed from time to time of men who are trusted because they are seen to have "a connexion with the interest . . . the sentiments and opinions of the people."

George III's slogan, "not men, but measures," was pernicious precisely because consent is in large part the consequence of confidence in, and identification with, men. "The laws reach but a little way. Constitute government how you please, infinitely the greater part of it must depend upon the exercise of the powers which are left at large to the prudence and uprightness of ministers of state." Consent will not long be yielded to faceless officials, or to mere servants of one man, who themselves have no "connexion with the interest of the people." In opposing the cant of "not men, but measures," Burke therefore resisted rule by nonparty ministers who lacked the confidence of the Commons. By the same token we may today oppose excessive White House staff-government by private men whom Congress never sees. It was not for nothing that the American Constitution provided for "executive Departments" and for Senate confirmation of the appointments of great officers of state.

Safeguards against arbitrary power, resistance to total power, assurance of stable government which is responsive and capable of generating long-term consent—these are agnostic objectives. Any true believer will want total power to achieve the true ends of government, and will be a democrat or an authoritarian depending, as Burke said, on which scheme or system he thinks will bring him nearer to total power. But any thoroughgoing agnostic might well also be a radical democrat, believing that nothing matters and that the merest whim of the majority is as good a guide to social action as anything else; and perhaps this is simply another form of true belief, like reliance on astrology or oracles. In any case Burke was neither a true believer nor a thoroughgoing agnostic. He was a Christian, and if anything something of a mystic, but no ideologue.

True believers—though not Christians—theorists, and ideologues made the French Revolution, and for Burke a politics of theory and ideology, of abstract, absolute ideas was an abomination, whether the idea was the right of the British Parliament to tax the American colonies or the rights of man. Such a politics cannot work as politics. It begins and ends by sacrificing peace, and it must proceed from one bloodbath to another and from one tyranny to another. Ideas are the inventions of men and are as arbitrary as their will. The business of politics is not with theory and ideology but with accommodation. "All government, indeed every human benefit and enjoyment," Burke said in 1775 urging conciliation with America, "every virtue, and every prudent act, is founded on compromise and barter. We balance inconveniences; we give and take; we remit some rights, that we may enjoy others; and we choose rather to be happy citizens, than subtle disputants." He would not enter into "distinctions of rights . . . these metaphysical distinctions; I hate the very sound of them." They were, he found later, what the French Revolution was about. These revolutionaries build their politics, he wrote in the *Appeal from the New to the Old Whigs*, a year after the *Reflections*, "not on convenience but on truth; and they profess to conduct men to a certain happiness by the assertion of their undoubted rights. With them there is no compromise. . . . Their principles always go to the extreme."

The presumption, the arrogance of these Frenchmen's assurance in their new discovery, appalled Burke. Those "rights of man" were an invitation to another round of religious wars and persecutions, not likely to be any the less fanatical or bloody for the irreligiousness of the new dogma. "The foundation of government is . . . not in imaginary rights of men," Burke argued, "but in political convenience, and in human nature. . . ." Government thus stops short "of some hazardous or ambiguous excellence," but it is the better for it.

Men do have rights, Burke wrote in the *Reflections*, but as civil society is made for the advantage of man, "all the advantages for which it is made become his right." The rights of man, this is to say, have no independent, theoretical existence. They do not preexist and condition civil society. They are in their totality the right to decent, wise, just, responsive, stable government in the circumstances of a given time and place. Under such a government, a partnership Burke calls it, "the restraints on men, as well as their liberties, are to be reckoned among their rights," and "all men have equal rights, but not to equal things," since a leveling egalitarianism which does not reward merit and ability is harmful to all and is unjust as well.

Civil society is a creature of its past, of "a great mysterious incorporation," and of an evolution which in improving never produces anything "wholly new," and in conserving never retains anything "wholly obsolete." It may malfunction—the English constitution did in 1688—and then drastic measures may be called for to restore it to its true self, but that true self ought never be altered, and certainly society ought never be uprooted, never be razed to the ground and replaced with some wholly new construct. This passionately held faith and his deprecation of the rights of man form the basis of Burke's reputation as the purveyor of a conservative doctrine unfit for modern consumption, as the last apologist for an oppressive social order now long dead and unlamented, as an obscurantist reactionary, an opponent not only of humanitarian reform but of reason itself.

To be sure, the conservative reputation does not fit the Whig of the 1770s and '80s, the advocate of consent and limited power, the friend of the American Revolution, or even the critic of the totalitarian tendencies of the French Revolution. But Burke's contemporary adversaries and his later detractors get around that by accusing him of having abandoned his earlier convictions. He got frightened, he got old, his sympathy dried up, he went Tory, perhaps he was not even altogether of sound mind. John Morley's opinion, however—and Morley was critical of much in the *Reflections*—was that Burke "changed his front, but he never changed his ground,"[12] and this opinion can be shown to be

12. Morley, *Burke*, p. 169.

correct. The same principles, the same "uniform scheme and rule of life" that informed the earlier Whig animated the author of the *Reflections*. The latter work is, therefore, not to be so simply rejected. "Fly from the French Revolution," Burke cried in Parliament in 1791.[13] The liberal tradition did not fly from the revolution. It fled from Burke instead, and that was a mistake.

Of course there are moments in the *Reflections* that are nothing but sterile reaction. There is the passage that Tom Paine tellingly picked up in which Burke makes love to Marie Antionette, that "Roman matron," and laments that "the age of chivalry is gone . . . gone—that . . . charity of honor which felt a stain like a wound . . . which ennobled whatever it touched, and under which vice itself lost half its evil by losing all its grossness."[14] With this passage, says Sir Philip Magnus, "the Romantic Movement in English literature had begun,"[15] which is certainly too bad. But even here Burke exaggerates a valid point, namely that manners, civility, certain forms and standards of behavior, what he calls the "public affections," are founded in custom and are all easily exploded by a shallow reason. They are nothing but "pleasing illusions which made power gentle and obedience liberal"; they are "the decent drapery of life." But without them society and government are brutal, conflict is naked. It is all too easy and it is fatal to keep tearing them off until not only is a king merely a man and a queen just a woman, but also "a woman is but an animal, and an animal not of the highest order."

Again there is the passage where we are told that the poor must be trained to obedience and labor, "and when they find, as they commonly do, the success disproportioned to the endeavor, they must be taught their consolation in the final proportions of eternal justice." Not an edifying sentence. But Burke had a social conscience, if a perplexed one. He puzzled, with feeling, over how to rescue people doomed to "servile, degrading, unseemly, unmanly . . . unwholesome . . . pestiferous occupations" but asked, "What is the use of discussing a man's abstract right to food or

13. Quoted in Magnus, *Burke*, p. 218.
14. Ibid., pp. 196, 198.
15. Ibid., p. 198.

medicine? The question is upon the method of procuring, and administering them." And yet again Burke surely treated much too lightly the abuses of the French monarchy, aristocracy, and clergy, and the misery they bred. France needed a revolution, if anything more than England in 1688 or America in 1776, though not the one it got, and Burke should have seen this. Nor, finally, was Burke without his share of anti-Semitism, though it was of a variety that barely rises to the notice of anyone who has lived through the first half of the twentieth century.

But all this cannot on any fair reading be taken as central to the *Reflections*, and much will be missed by those who do so take it. First there is in the worst, as it might be viewed, of Burke's so-called conservatism a powerful realism that any political thought denies or ignores at its peril. You cannot start from scratch, he maintained, and expect to produce anything but a continual round of chaos and tyranny, until you return to the remnants of what you sought to destroy. Perfection is unlikely in human contrivances, and so the professed purpose of any scheme that attempts to start fresh will be defeated. The old vices tend to reappear in new institutions if their causes have not been attacked, but only their outward manifestations, which were the old institutions. Meanwhile the price has been paid of teaching men to yield as little respect to new institutions as was shown for the old, and, in a continual round of change, men unmoored from their past "become little better than the flies of summer." Even in pursuit of the most radical reforming ends, it is, moreover, simple practical common sense "to make the most of the existing materials." A politician, Burke lectured—contemplating in sheer unbelieving wonder the destruction of the church in France and the confiscation and dismantling of productive church property—a politician, "to do great things, looks for a *power*, what our workmen call a *purchase*." Here, in the church, were revenues, here was a bureaucracy. To destroy all this and scatter it rather than to use it seemed to Burke the height of stupidity—and subsequent French history proved him right. In the same spirit, reading Condorcet's dictum that the American Constitution "had not grown, but was planned," that it had taken no weight from the centuries but was put together mechanically in a few years, John Adams commented in the margin: "Fool! Fool!"[16]

Continuity—a practical necessity, if nothing else—was for Burke the principle of reform, not of opposition to it. Even revolutionary reform, as in England in 1688 and in America a century later, might be called for by a "grave and overruling necessity," in order to conserve by correcting. But the science of government is practical and intended for practical purposes. Cause and effect are most often obscure, and it is, therefore, "with infinite caution that any man ought to venture upon pulling down an edifice which has answered in any tolerable degree for ages the common purposes of society." This is conservatism, no doubt, but what is behind it is not wish, or tired old age, or romantic delusion, or moral obtuseness, or class interest, but good practical wisdom.

Burke's conservatism, however, served another purpose as well. In order to survive, be coherent and stable, and answer to men's wants, a civil society had to rest on a foundation of moral values. Else it degenerated—if an oligarchy, into interest government, a government of jobbers enriching themselves and their friends, and ended in revolution; or if a full democracy, into a mindless, shameless thing, freely oppressing various minorities and ruining itself. Burke's pragmatism, strong as it is, did not go to the length of taking mind out of politics. Metaphysics, yes; mind and values, no. But where are a society's values to be found? In theory? Metaphysics, abstract rights, would always clash with men's needs and their natures, and with various unforeseeable contingencies.

Theories were not fit to live with, and any attempt to impose them would breed conflict, not responsive government enjoying the consent of the governed. The rights of man cannot be established by any theoretical definition; they are "in balances between differences of good, in compromises sometimes between good and evil, and sometimes between evil and evil. Political reason

16. Quoted in Louis Hartz, *The Liberal Tradition in America* (New York: Harcourt, Brace and Co., 1955), p. 49.

is a computing principle: adding, substracting, multiplying, and dividing, morally and not metaphysically, or mathematically, true moral denominations." The visions of good and evil, the denominations to be computed—these a society draws from its past and without them it dies. Burke was strong for the union of church and state, since he viewed religion as a major source of the values that held a society together. He even praised, on the same score, the ancient prejudices of the people, using the word in a somewhat different sense from the way we do, and warned against exchanging the people's old superstitions—"the religion of feeble minds"—for new.

For many millions of us, organized religion no longer plays the role Burke assigned to it, and we want nothing of superstition and prejudice. Burke may have regretted the Enlightenment, but it did occur. The Age of Reason continues, if not quite as pretentiously and self-confidently as it began. Precisely for that reason, however, the problem to which Burke spoke is even more acute for us. A valueless politics and valueless institutions are shameful and shameless and, what is more, man's nature is such that he finds them, and life with and under them, insupportable. Doctrinaire theories of the rights of man, on the other hand, serve us no better than Burke thought they would. The computing principle is still all we can resort to, and we always return to it following some luxuriant outburst of theory in the Supreme Court, whether the theory is of an absolute right to contract, or to speak, or to stand mute, or to be private. We find our visions of good and evil and the denominations we compute where Burke told us to look, in the experience of the past, in our tradition, in the secular religion of the American republic. The only abiding thing, as Brandeis used to repeat and as Burke might not have denied, is change, but the past should control it, or at least its pace. We hold to the values of the past provisionally only, in the knowledge that they will change, but we hold to them as guides.

This is not, as Holmes once remarked, a duty, it is a necessity. How else are we to know anything? What is the use of empty "rationalists," such as were discovered at many a university some years ago, who being confronted with various demands for instant change, found that they believed nothing and could not judge any change as better or worse than another? They drove the very seekers after change up the wall in frustration. Nobody wants everybody not to believe in anything. And who wants politicians who, as Burke said, "see no merit or demerit in any man, or any action, or any political principle" except in terms of a desired political end, and who "therefore take up, one day, the most violent and stretched prerogative, and another time the wildest democratic ideas of freedom, and pass from one to the other."

Our problem, as much as Burke's, is that we cannot govern, and should not, in submission to the dictates of abstract theories, and that we cannot live, much less govern, without some "uniform rule and scheme of life," without principles, however provisionally and skeptically held. Burke's conservatism, if that is what it was, belongs to the liberal tradition, properly understood and translated to our time.

The Supreme Court and Evolving Principle

Since few principles are inscribed sharply in the Constitution itself, the Supreme Court speaking in the name of the Constitution fills, in part, the need for middle-distance principles that Burke described. It proffers, with some important exceptions, a series of admonitions, an eighteenth-century checklist of subjects; it does this cautiously and with some skepticism. It recognizes that principles are necessary, have evolved, and should continue to evolve in the light of history and changing circumstance. That—and not Hugo Black's—is the Constitution as the Framers wrote it. And that is what it must be in a secular democratic society, where the chief reliance for policy-making is placed in the political process.

The Constitution, said Justice Holmes in a famous dissent in 1905,[17] "is made for people of fundamentally differing views." Few definite, comprehensive answers on matters of social and

17. Lochner v. New York, 198 U.S. 45 (1905).

economic policy can be deduced from it. The judges, themselves abstracted from, removed from political institutions by several orders of magnitude, ought never to impose an answer on the society merely because it seems prudent and wise to them personally, or because they believe that an answer—always provisional —arrived at by the political institutions is foolish. The Court's first obligation is to move cautiously, straining for decisions in small compass, more hesitant to deny principles held by some segments of the society than ready to affirm comprehensive ones for all, mindful of the dominant role the political institutions are allowed, and always anxious first to invent compromises and accommodations before declaring firm and unambiguous principles.

Yet in the end, and even if infrequently, we do expect the Court to give us principle, the limits of which can be sensed but not defined and are communicated more as cautions than as rules. Confined to a profession, the explication of principle is disciplined, imposing standards of analytical candor, rigor, and clarity. The Court is to reason, not feel, to explain and justify principles it pronounces to the last possible rational decimal point. It may not itself generate values, out of the stomach, but must seek to relate them—at least analogically—to judgments of history and moral philosophy. We tend to think of the Court as deciding, but more often than not it merely ratifies or, what is even less, does *not* disapprove, or less still, decides not to decide. And even when it does take it upon itself to strike a balance of values, it does so with an ear to the promptings of the past and an eye strained to a vision of the future much more than with close regard to the present. Burke's description of an evolution meets the case: to produce nothing wholly new and retain nothing wholly obsolete. The function is canalized by the adversary process, which limits the occasions of judgment and tends to structure issues and narrow their scope to manageable proportions.

In 1905, when Holmes wrote the *Lochner* dissent, the justices were grinding out annual answers to social and economic questions on the basis of personal convictions of what was wise— derived, as it happens, from the laissez-faire philosophy of Herbert Spencer. That would not do, Holmes told them, and it did not, although it took thirty years for a majority of the justices to see it, and Holmes was gone by then. None has reread Herbert Spencer into the Constitution since, but in the 1960s a majority of the justices, under Earl Warren, again began to dictate answers to social and sometimes economic problems. The problems were different—not regulation of economic enterprise, not labor relations, but the structure of politics, educational policy, the morals and mores of the society. And the answers were differently derived, not from Spencer's Social Statics, but from fashionable notions of progress. Again, it may take time before the realization comes that this will not do.

On January 22, 1973, the Supreme Court, paying formal tribute to Holmes's 1905 dissent but violating its spirit, undertook to settle the abortion issue.[18] In place of the various state abortion statutes in controversy and in flux, the Supreme Court prescribed a virtually uniform statute of its own. During the first three months of pregnancy, the Court decreed, a woman and her physician may decide on an abortion quite free of any interference by the state, except as the state requires the physician to be licensed; during the second three months the state may impose health regulations, but not forbid abortion; during the last three months, the state may if it chooses forbid as well as regulate. That may be a wise model statute, although there is considerable question why the Court foreclosed state regulation of the places where the abortion is to be performed. The state regulates and licenses restaurants and pool halls and Turkish baths and God knows what else in order to protect the public; why may it not similarly regulate and license abortion clinics, or doctors' offices where abortions are to be performed?

But if the Court's model statute is generally intelligent, what is the justification for its imposition? If this statute, why not one on proper grounds of divorce, or on adoption of children? Medical evidence, the Court tells us now, shows that abortions during the first three months of pregnancy present no great risk. Well

18. Roe v. Wade, 410 U.S. 113 (1973); Doe v. Bolton, 410 U.S. 179 (1973).

and good. It is also clear that the fetus is not a life in being at the early stages of pregnancy, is not entitled to constitutional protection, and the Constitution cannot be construed to forbid abortion. Well and good again. But the fetus is a potential life, and the Court acknowledges that society has a legitimate interest in it. So has the individual—the mother, and one would suppose also the father; an interest that may be characterized as a claim to personal privacy, which in some contexts the Constitution has been found to protect. The individual's interest, here, overrides society's interest in the first three months and, subject only to health regulations, also in the second; in the third trimester, society is preeminent.

One is left to ask why. The Court never said. It refused the discipline to which its function is properly subject. It simply asserted the result it reached. This is all the Court could do because moral philosophy, logic, reason, or other materials of law can give no answer. If medical considerations only were involved, a satisfactory rational answer might be arrived at. But, as the Court acknowledged, they are not. Should not the question then have been left to the political process, which in state after state can achieve not one but many accommodations, adjusting them from time to time as attitudes change? It is astonishing that only two dissented from the Court's decision, although Justice Potter Stewart noted in his agreement, presumably with some discomfort, that the decision joined the long line of earlier cases imposing judicially made social policy to which Holmes had objected.[19] The dissenters were Justices Byron White and William Rehnquist. The Court's decision was an "extravagant exercise" of judicial power, said Justice White;[20] it was a legislative rather than judicial action, suggested Justice Rehnquist.[21] So it was, and if the Court's guess on the probable and desirable direction of progress is wrong, that guess will nevertheless have been imposed on all fifty states. Normal legislation, enacted by legislatures not judges,

19. Roe v. Wade, 410 U.S. at 167.
20. Doe v. Bolton, 410 U.S. at 221 (White, J., dissenting from *Roe* and *Doe*).
21. Roe v. Wade, 410 U.S. at 171.

is happily less rigid and less presumptuous in claims to universality and permanence. The claim to universality and permanence is illusory, in any case, for the ongoing political process which follows upon the declaration of law is another discipline the Court is subject to. Yet the Court is not excused in transgressing all limits, in refusing its own prior discipline, for in its initial process of law formation the Court is not under the discipline of the political process. Neither the Court nor its principles directly originate there. The discipline is subsequent.

Such is the Court's function under the constitution of open texture, as it is aptly called. There is another constitution as well; I will call it the manifest constitution; it is the constitution of structure and process, not of due process or equal protection, and certainly not of metaphysical privileges and immunities. More theory has to be poured into it than can be extracted; it is the constitution of the mechanics of institutional arrangements and of the political process, of power allocation and the division of powers, and the historically defined hard core of procedural provisions, found chiefly in the Bill of Rights. These hard-core provisions, as Felix Frankfurter once wrote, have a relative "definiteness of terms" and "definiteness of history," derived from the specific grievances the Framers meant to redress.[22] In establishing the power of judicial review in 1803, in *Marbury* v. *Madison*,[23] vesting the Supreme Court with value-definition exercised in the name of the Constitution, John Marshall spoke of the Constitution as law, and reasoned that when properly invoked before them in a case judges must enforce it. He spoke as if most of it were manifest, and suggested later that where it is open-textured it confers little if any power on judges. Matters have turned out quite the other way around. The judges have little to do with the manifest constitution; they chiefly exercise power by invoking its open texture. But Marshall was right in his view that the manifest constitution is law, and a special kind of law at that, imposing a

22. Felix Frankfurter, *Law and Politics*, ed. Edward F. Prichard, Jr. and Archibald MacLeish (New York: Harcourt, Brace and Co., 1939), pp. 10, 12.
23. Marbury v. Madison, 5 U.S. (1 Cranch) 137 (1803).

duty to obey of the sort that does not definitely attach, except broadly in the aggregate, to other general law in our system, and imposing it most particularly on all officers of government, state and federal, who by article VI are oath-bound to support the Constitution.

There is a moral duty, and there ought to be, for those to whom it is applicable—most often officers of government—to obey the manifest constitution, unless and until it is altered by the amendment process it itself provides for, a duty analogous to the duty to obey final judicial decrees. No president may decide to stay in office for a term of six years rather than four, or, since the Twenty-second Amendment, to run for a third term. There is an absolute duty to obey; to disobey is to deny the idea of constitutionalism, that special kind of law which establishes a set of pre-existing rules within which society works out all its other rules from time to time. To deny this idea is in the most fundamental sense to deny the idea of law itself.

The liberal contractarian tradition, as Justice Black represented it, posits a duty to obey judicial decrees, and beyond that a duty to obey the manifest constitution, and a further duty to obey the general law the Court makes in the open texture. And yet the manifest constitution presents problems, just as popular sovereignty does in its way. For the contractarian liberal is a moralist, and the moralist will find it difficult to sacrifice his aims in favor of structure and process, to sacrifice substance for form. Yet process and form, which is the embodiment of process, are the essence of the theory and practice of constitutionalism.

I have shared and do share the tendency of the liberal imagination to respect the moral claims of justice against the status quo. I insist more strongly, even passionately, quite as if I were talking about justice, on a politics of the computing principle, which Burke urged upon us. It seems to me to make everything else possible. Without it, in the stark universe of imperatives, in the politics of ideal promises and inevitable betrayals, justice is not merely imperfect, as under the computing principle, but soon becomes injustice.

2

Citizen or Person?
What Is Not Granted
Cannot Be Taken Away

2

Citizen or Person?
What Is Not Granted
Cannot Be Taken Away

In the view both of the ancients and of modern liberal political theorists, the relationship between the individual and the state is largely defined by the concept of citizenship. It is by virtue of his citizenship that the individual is a member of the political community, and by virtue of it that he has rights. Remarkably enough—and as I will suggest, happily—the concept of citizenship plays only the most minimal role in the American constitutional scheme.

Citizenship, Professor Michael Walzer has written, "itself has become a problem."[1] I'm not sure what that means and I'm not sure that I subscribe to its somewhat apocalyptic tone. Yet there is something in it. One remembers a time not long gone when patriotism was a word in common usage and of definite and widely accepted meaning. For many people it plainly is not today.

The patriot may be the exaggerated or emotional citizen, but the concept of citizenship, whatever the malaise that may now afflict it, has been central nonetheless to much of ancient and modern political thought. A person's relationship to the law and the duty to obey law, while not necessarily exhausted by the concept of citizenship, is surely tied to it. Aristotle asked, What is a

---

1. Michael Walzer, *Obligations: Essays on Disobedience, War and Citizenship* (Cambridge: Harvard University Press, 1970), p. 204.

state? and replied that it is the citizens who compose it. Who is a citizen, he said, will vary with the form of government, whether oligarchy or democracy—a tyranny presumably has no citizens. A citizen is not simply a resident. Aliens, though resident, are not citizens, nor are slaves. "He who has the power to take part in the deliberative or judicial administration of any state is said by us to be a citizen of that state; and speaking generally, a state is a body of citizens sufficing for the purposes of life."[2] Modern thinkers, and particularly liberal ones, generally set no less store by the concept of citizenship. Lockean contractarian doctrine, proceeding as it does from natural rights, is not, as might appear, universalist; it is intended to support and justify the national, constitutional state. The notion of contract presupposes parties, and the parties are citizens.

There is a great deal to the Hobbesian notion that we are all really subjects held to obedience, if no longer by divine command then by a simple fear of our fellows. To the extent that this explanation does not fit our situation or ought not, to the extent that it is not the true or the good explanation, liberal as well as classic thought has considered us citizens who owe obedience, as we owe allegiance, chiefly because we are self-governing, and as self-governing because we are citizens. When they freed themselves from subjection, the makers of the French Revolution called each other citizen, denoting their participation in the state; so the communists later called each other comrade, denoting their common allegiance to an ideology, a movement.

Both classic and later liberal statements of the duty to obey law thus subsume the concept of citizenship, even though not as a wholly necessary or sufficient condition. Also subsumed are the clarity and economy of the law to be obeyed, and of the process by which that law is formed. The classic among classics is, of course, the statement of Socrates as reported in the *Crito*: "In war as in the court of justice, and everywhere, you must do whatever your state and your country tell you to do, or you must persuade

2. Walzer, *Obligations*, pp. 205 et seq.

them that their commands are unjust." It is the citizen who has the standing to persuade his fellow citizens that what they are doing is unjust. Our own system does not resemble the one subsumed in the statement of Socrates in clarity or in economy of application, and not in the immediacy with which the citizen can affect the process of law-formation. That makes a difference; so, also, although less directly and certainly, does the striking ambivalence, the great ambiguity that has surrounded the concept of citizenship in our law and in our tradition.

The original Constitution, prior to Reconstruction, contained no definition of citizenship and precious few references to the concept altogether. The subject was not entirely ignored by the Framers. They empowered Congress to make a uniform rule of naturalization. But, wishing to attract immigrants, they rejected nativist suggestions for strict naturalization requirements, such as long residence.[3] They plainly assumed that birth as well as naturalization would confer citizenship but they made nothing depend on it explicitly, aside from a few offices: president, congressman, senator, but notably not judge. State citizenship provided one, but only one of several, means of access to federal courts (under the diversity jurisdiction) and conferred the not unqualified right, under the privileges and immunities clause of article IV, section 2, to be treated generally by each state in the same fashion as its own citizens were treated. Discrimination on the sole ground of not holding citizenship in a given state is forbidden; discrimination on other and reasonable grounds is, however, allowed. Discriminations on the basis of residence, which is different in concept from citizenship, are permitted; and where state citizenship is a reasonable requirement, as for officeholding, discrimination is not prohibited. But if no special reason restricts a privilege sensibly to the state's own citizens, the state must extend it to the citizens of other states as well.

There is no further mention of citizenship in the Constitution

3. See Frank George Franklin, *The Legislative History of Naturalization in the United States* (New York: Arno Press, 1969), chap. 2.

before the Civil War amendments, even though there were plenty
of occasions for making rights depend on it. The Preamble speaks
of "We the people of the United States," not, as it might have, of
we the citizens of the United States at the time of the formation
of this union. And the Bill of Rights throughout defines rights of
people, not of citizens. In the First Amendment, it is "the right
of the people peaceably to assemble," in the Second, "the right
of the people to keep and bear arms," whatever that might mean.
And so on. No wonder, then, that citizenship was nowhere defined in the original Constitution. It was not important. Under
English law, to which the Framers were accustomed, citizenship
was conferred automatically by birth, but the Framers undoubtedly assumed that citizenship did not necessarily run with the
blood as it did in English law. And while under English law the
status was indelible—once a subject, always a subject, and under
rather heavy obligations—the men who made our revolution had
broken away from that subjection: they did not believe, as they
soon demonstrated, in the indelible, inalienable status of citizenship: and they were prepared to receive and naturalize immigrants
similarly willing to shed previously inalienable states of subjection. To be sure, implicitly, the citizen had a right freely to enter
the country, whereas the alien did not; and implicitly also the
citizen, while abroad, could be held to an obligation of allegiance
and might under very specific conditions be found guilty of the
crime of treason for violating it, while the alien generally could
not. But these were hardly critical points, as the Framers demonstrated by saying nothing explicit about them. It remains true that
the original Constitution presented the edifying picture of a
government that bestowed rights on people and persons, and held
itself out as bound by certain standards of conduct in its relations
with people and persons, not with some legal construct called
citizen. This idyllic state of affairs was rudely disturbed by the
crisis of the 1850s. Like so much else, it foundered on the contradiction of slavery. A majority of the Supreme Court seized on
the concept of citizenship in the *Dred Scott* case,[4] in a futile and

4. Scott v. Sandford, 60 U.S. (19 Howard) 393 (1857).

misguided effort, by way of a legalism and an unfounded legalism at that, to resolve the controversy over the spread of slavery.

Dred Scott, the slave of one John Sandford in Missouri, brought suit in the Circuit Court of the United States for his freedom. As the law of Missouri provided for trying questions of personal freedom, Sandford, in effect, was assumed to hold a piece of property, and Scott claimed that Sandford held it unlawfully because he, Scott, owned it. That is to say, Scott sued to recover himself. It was as if he were a chattel somebody had wrongfully taken from him.—I, not this man who is holding me, own me. The ground on which Dred Scott claimed title to himself was this: A predecessor owner had taken Scott from Missouri to Illinois— a free state—and from there into the Upper Louisiana territory, north of the latitude 36 degrees and 30 minutes north—also free, under the Compromise of 1820. So Scott had lived in free territory and in a free state for some years before being returned to Missouri. Scott claimed that freedom is infectious, and that he had caught it. However, Scott could come into federal court only by claiming to be a citizen of Missouri; Sandford, who held Scott in Missouri, was himself a citizen of New York. Scott could not be a citizen of Missouri, Sandford said, because he was "a negro of African descent, whose ancestors were of pure African blood, and who were brought into this country and sold as slaves." If Scott was not a citizen of Missouri, there could be no federal jurisdiction, and that was an end of the matter. The significance of citizenship was in question. The lower court held that Scott could be a citizen, but that freedom was not infectious and that Scott had not caught it.

In the Supreme Court the majority opinion was written by Chief Justice Roger Taney, Marshall's successor, a figure not without precedent in our history and not without successors. A line of Turgenev's *Fathers and Sons* refers to a character as "at once progressive (in the political sense) and a despot, as often happens with Russians." It has happened in this country, and it happened with Taney, a political progressive—if that is a correct designation for a Jacksonian populist—an economic liberal, and a racist who persuaded himself by mid-life that slavery was not

only a necessary evil, if that, but right as well. Taney combined
personal kindness with public ferocity, he freed his own slaves and
cared for them afterward, but he was opposed politically to any
large-scale manumission. He was an able man, broken on the
rack of slavery. Dred Scott, Taney held, could not be a citizen,
not because he was a slave but because, even if he were a free
man, he was "a negro of African descent, whose ancestors were
of pure African blood, and who were brought into this country
and sold as slaves." The words "people of the United States" and
"citizens" are synonymous terms, he held, used interchangeably
in the Constitution: "They both describe the political body who,
according to our republican institutions, form the sovereignty,
and who hold the power and conduct the government through
their representatives. They are what we familiarly call the
[single] 'sovereign people' and every citizen is one of this people,
and a constituent member of this sovereignty."[5]

At the time of the framing of the Constitution Taney continued,
even free Negroes were not viewed as being a portion of "this
people," the constituent membership of the sovereignty. They
were not viewed as citizens or as entitled to any of the rights and
privileges the Constitution held out to citizens. In this Taney was
probably wrong, as the dissenters, I think, demonstrated. Taney's
Constitution held out rights and privileges to citizens, even though
the document itself holds out few to citizens as such, does not
bother to define the status of citizenship, and altogether appears
to set very little store by it. Taney, by an *ipse dixit*, argued that
when the Constitution says "people" it means the same thing as
citizens. Yet the Constitution says citizens rarely, and people most
of the time, and never the two interchangeably.

When the Constitution was formed, Taney said, Negroes were
"considered as a subordinate and inferior class of beings, who
had been subjugated by the dominant race, and, whether eman-
cipated or not, yet remained subject to their authority, and had no
rights or privileges but such as those who held the power and the

5. Ibid. at 404.

Government might choose to grant them."[6] Now, this is a perversion of the complex, guilt-ridden, and highly ambivalent attitude of the Framers toward slavery, and of their vague, and possibly evasive and culpably less than candid expectation of some future evolution away from it. It is possible to have some compassion for the Framers in their travail over the contradiction of slavery. It is not possible to have compassion for Taney's hardening of the Framers' position, his stripping it of its original aspirations to decency as well as of its illusions, and his reattribution to the Framers of the position thus altered. He claimed "that unfortunate race" was "regarded as beings of an inferior order, and altogether unfit to associate with the white race, either in social or political relations; and so far inferior, that they had no rights which the white man was bound to respect; and that the negro might justly and lawfully be reduced to slavery for his benefit."[7] The Negro had no rights which the white man is bound to respect. This sentence became a political slogan of the abolitionists and the Republicans, and one can take some satisfaction in knowing that it shocked the conscience and the expectations of good majorities outside the South, and perhaps in the South itself. They thought it brutal and totally unacceptable. If the Negro, as Taney said, "was bought and sold, and treated as an ordinary article of merchandise and traffic, whenever profit could be made by it," how, then, could he be a citizen? Well, no doubt the troubled men who wrote the Constitution tolerated the buying and selling of human beings, but it is not true that their thought was as consistent and brutal as Taney made it out to be. They expected, in some measure fatuously perhaps, to redeem themselves. "I tremble for my country," said Jefferson, "when I think that God

6. Ibid. at 404–5. The Framers intended that state citizenship could be conferred on free Negroes, Taney said, but Negroes were not thereby entitled to any rights of citizens of the United States. He and his majority further decreed that the Compromise of 1820 was unconstitutional. The point was central to the great national debate which followed. The Lincoln-Douglas debates chiefly turned on it.

7. Ibid. at 407.

is just." Yet Taney denied the possibility of any process of redemption under this Constitution, and appealed for good measure to an unjust God.

The original Constitution's innocence of the concept of citizenship was thus violated in the *Dred Scott* case, in an encounter with the contradiction of slavery. A rape having occurred, innocence could never be restored. But remarkably enough, after a period of reaction to the trauma, we resumed behaving as if our virginity were intact and with a fair measure of credibility at that. Fewer than four months after the Thirteenth Amendment became law, in December 1865, Congress enacted the Civil Rights Act of 1866. With the express intention of overruling *Dred Scott*, the act declared that "all persons born in the United States and not subject to any foreign power, excluding Indians not taxed, are hereby declared to be citizens of the United States."[8] This was the first authoritative definition of citizenship in American law. It had become necessary to make clear that race and descent from slaves was no ground of exclusion. For the first time, and for the same reason, *a set of rights* depending on citizenship was incidental. A previous version of the statute referred to inhabitants in conferring these new rights, rather than to citizens.[9] As it occurred to the draftsman that he had better make clear that Negroes could be citizens, it became a matter of ease in drafting also to define rights he was about to confer in terms of citizenship. The *Dred Scott* decision used the concept of citizenship negatively, as exclusionary. It indicated who was not under the umbrella of rights and privileges and status and thus entrenched the subjection of the Negro in the Constitution. The Civil Rights Act of 1866 was equally negative; *Dred Scott* had to be exorcised. In the process, as a matter of syntactic compulsion, of stylistic necessity, as a matter of the flow of the pen, the concept of citizenship was revived.

When the same Congress that passed the 1866 Civil Rights

8. Civil Rights Act of April 9, 1866, ch. 31, § 1, 14 Stat. 27.
9. See Charles Fairman, "Reconstruction and Reunion 1864–88," *History of the Supreme Court of the United States* (New York: Macmillan Co., 1971), 6: 1172.

Act wrote the Fourteenth Amendment, it forbade any state to "abridge the privileges or immunities of citizens of the United States." The author of this phrase was John A. Bingham, a Representative from Ohio, a Republican of abolitionist antecedents. He was a type that frequently occurred in our political life, a man of enthusiastic rhetorical bent, on the whole of generous impulse, and of zero analytical inclination or capacity. A Republican colleague in the House recalling quite specifically the privileges and immunities clause, and that it came from Bingham, said: "Its euphony and indefiniteness of meaning were a charm to him."[10] The only explanation of this clause that was attempted in the long course of the congressional debate on the amendment came from Bingham, and it confirms his contemporaries' estimate of him—it was highly confused. As an afterthought, by amendment in the Senate of the text passed in the House, a definition of citizenship modeled on the Civil Rights Act of 1866 was added: "All persons born or naturalized in the United States and subject to the jurisdiction thereof [which may exclude the children of foreign ambassadors, and means little, if anything, more than that], are citizens of the United States and of the state wherein they reside."

The *Dred Scott* decision had to be effectively, which is to say constitutionally, overruled by a definition of citizenship in which race played no part. So, in a fashion no one quite understood but everyone apparently found necessary, *Dred Scott* was exorcised. That having been done, the rest of section 1 of the Fourteenth Amendment made no further reference to citizens. And the distinction between citizens and persons did not go unnoticed. Senator Howard pointed out that the due process and equal protection clauses "disable a State from depriving not merely a citizen of the United States, but any person, . . . of life, liberty, or property without due process of law, or from denying to him the equal protection of the laws of the State."[11]

At this stage of our history we stood at a point where the status

10. Ibid., p. 1270.
11. Ibid., p. 1295.

of citizenship might have become all-important, not because of a deliberate, reasoned decision, but owing to the particular dialectic of the *Dred Scott* case, which one may view as an accident, and of the natural reaction to it. Actually, the concept of citizenship, once inserted in the Fourteenth Amendment, survived as a drafting technique in three later constitutional amendments which safeguard the right to vote against particular infringements. But on the whole the development was away from this concept—owing to yet another accident.

This other accident was the decision in the *Slaughter-House Cases*[12] of 1873, in which the Supreme Court for the first time construed the newly enacted Fourteenth Amendment. The first reading of the great Reconstruction amendment had nothing to do with Negroes, slavery, civil rights, or in any other way with the aftermath of the Civil War. The case arose instead out of a more than ordinarily corrupt enactment of the Louisiana legislature in 1869, which created a slaughtering monopoly in New Orleans. In retrospect, one never ceases to be astonished that the Fourteenth Amendment should have been regarded as relevant to a controversy about butchering in New Orleans. But it did occur to one of counsel for the butchers: John A. Campbell, a former justice of the Supreme Court of the United States and a member of the majority that decided the *Dred Scott* case, an opponent of secession on political grounds, who—alone among the Southern justices—had thought it his duty to resign when his state seceded. Campbell argued that the Fourteenth Amendment, "with an imperial authority," had defined national citizenship and had made it primary. The privileges of a citizen of the United States must include the right "to cultivate the ground, or to purchase products, or to carry on trade, or to maintain himself and his family by free industry".[13] All this eloquence went for nought. Campbell's clients lost. "The banded butchers are busted," Matthew Hale Carpenter, counsel for the monopoly, wired *his* clients.[14] The Fourteenth Amendment had wrought a "mighty

12. Slaughter-House Cases, 83 U.S. (16 Wallace) 36 (1874).
13. Fairman, "Reconstruction and Reunion," p. 1345.
14. Ibid., p. 1349.

revolution" in the Constitution, as Campbell had said; it had created "great endowments of privilege, immunity, of right,"[15] as he claimed, but they were not to depend on citizenship.

The main purpose of the Fourteenth Amendment's definition of citizenship, Justice Samuel F. Miller began for the Court, was to overrule the *Dred Scott* case and "to establish the citizenship of the negro."[16] In addition, the definition clarified what Miller thought was a previously open but hardly world-shaking question: whether a person born not in a state, but in a territory or in the District of Columbia, who was therefore not a citizen of any state, could be a citizen of the United States. He could be. The Fourteenth Amendment made sure there would be no limbo.

But what could be meant by privileges and immunities of citizens of the United States? The sole purpose of the privileges and immunities clause of the original Constitution, article IV, section 2, said Justice Miller, was "to declare to the several States, that whatever those rights, as you grant or establish them to your own citizens, or as you limit or qualify or impose restrictions on their exercise, the same, neither more nor less, shall be the measure of rights of citizens of other States within your jurisdiction."[17] But the rights themselves did not depend on the federal government for their existence or protection. Their definition and their limitation lay within the power of the states.

Was the Fourteenth Amendment, by creating national citizenship, meant to work the radical change that Campbell had urged of making basic relationships between the individual and the state turn on federal law? If so, there had been a transfer from the state legislatures to Congress of the power to regulate economic and social conditions. For by section 5 of the Fourteenth Amendment Congress was given enforcement power. It could, therefore, legislate at will on virtually any such subject. What is more, power would be transferred not only to Congress but to the Supreme Court, which would be constituted "a perpetual censor upon all legislation of the states" dealing with social and economic

15. Ibid., p. 1346.
16. 83 U.S. (16 Wallace) at 73.
17. Ibid. at 77.

affairs, "with authority to nullify [any regulation enacted by a state that the Supreme Court] did not approve."[18] With the experience of a hundred years, we must call Miller's answer to Campbell's conception of national citizenship a liberal, a progressive answer, favoring majoritarian political power to enact social and economic regulation. Miller answered for the majority with a vigorous negative. The purpose of the privileges and immunities clause was to define, secure, and protect the citizenship of the newly freed slaves, that and no more. It was a close decision; the Court divided 5 to 4.

Was the privileges and immunities clause, then, entirely meaningless? Why did the draftsman put it in? We know why—because John A. Bingham liked the sound of it. But that is not good enough. Statutory and particularly constitutional enactments must be invested with some meaning, which Miller proceeded to do. National citizenship, he said, confers the right to come to the seat of government, a right protected for inanimate things, and for aliens as well, by the commerce clause; the right to seek (though probably not to claim) the protection of the government when outside the United States; the right to use the navigable waters of the United States, which under international law may be forbidden to aliens.[19] That was about it.

One day after the decision of the *Slaughter-House Cases*, the Court—unanimous now—disposed of the case of one Mrs. Myra Bradwell, an accomplished lawyer in Chicago who had been denied admission to the bar of the Illinois Supreme Court because she was a woman.[20] She said that this denial violated her privileges and immunities as a United States citizen. The Court said no. Justice Joseph Bradley in a concurring opinion to Miller's decision said, "The paramount mission and destiny of women are to fulfill the noble and benign offices of wife and mother. This is the law of the Creator. And the rules of civil society must be adapted to the general constitution of things, and cannot be based

18. Ibid. at 78.
19. Ibid. at 79.
20. Bradwell v. The State, 83 U.S. (16 Wallace) 130 (1872).

upon exceptional cases." A legislature was not obliged to permit women to practice law or, presumably, to pursue other careers which would make them independent of their husbands. A nice forecast, this, of what it would mean to have the Supreme Court sit as the ultimate censor of state social and economic legislation—a super-legislature resorting, if necessary, to the law of the Creator.

The Illinois legislature nevertheless changed its law, and Mrs. Bradwell was admitted to the bar of the Supreme Court of Illinois. Somewhat later, when a woman sought admission to the bar of the Supreme Court of the United States, admission was denied; tradition was so opposed that only a statute could effect a change, the chief justice said. But Congress did act, and in 1879 the first woman lawyer was admitted to the bar of the Supreme Court of the United States. The first black, moved by Charles Sumner of Massachusetts, had been admitted on February 1, 1865, with no problem at all.

The decision in the *Slaughter-House Cases*, however narrowly reached, has stuck so far as the argument proceeding from the privileges and immunities clause is concerned. And what it did was to bring us back to where we started. It concluded the flurry of the *Dred Scott* case, came around just about full circle, and left matters almost as they were before that episode. While we now have a definition of citizenship in the Constitution we still set very little store by it. But I said that this outcome, the closing of the circle, was again accidental or at least incidental, just as the exaltation of citizenship in *Dred Scott* was accidental or at least incidental. Justice Miller's *Slaughter-House* opinion—and in this Miller succeeded—just about read the privileges and immunities clause out of the Constitution. But Miller did what he did for reasons of federalism because he thought it important not to destroy the main features of the preexisting federal system, with its distribution of powers between state and federal governments, except as that distribution had been altered in order to secure rights for the newly freed Negro. That was the ground of decision, not that it would be wrong to make citizenship central to the relationship between the federal government and the people, not some philosophical notion about the proper role of the concept of citizenship.

All that Justice Miller strove to forestall did occur, if under a different formal rubric. The protection Campbell unsuccessfully claimed for his independent butchers in the *Slaughter-House Cases* under the privileges and immunities clause was later extended under the due process and equal protection clauses. A radical change in the theory of relations between the state and federal governments was accomplished, a departure from the structure and spirit of the original institutions. State governments were fettered and degraded by subjection to federal control, and the Court was constituted a perpetual censor upon all legislation of the states, with authority to nullify what it did not approve. For a season economic laissez-faire notions held sway, and the Court, invoking the due process and equal protection clauses, ruthlessly struck down social and economic regulations that the states attempted to enact; later it used the same clauses to effect somewhat broader and more humane ideas of social justice. The central purpose of the equal protection clause, posited by Miller as the sole purpose—to protect Negroes against racial discrimination—came to fruition more slowly.

The consequences of the decision in the *Slaughter-House Cases* with respect to the role played in our polity by the concept of citizenship have followed with inexorable logic. Although the Fifteenth, Nineteenth, and Twenty-sixth Amendments guarantee the right to vote in terms of citizenship, and the right to vote is now generally a function of United States citizenship, it was not always, and in some states not recently, so; and in any case it is not the Constitution that ties even that most symbolically charged act of participation in governance to the status of citizenship. There have been other, aberrant departures from the logic of the *Slaughter-House Cases*. But when challenged they are most often found to be insupportable contradictions, and are eliminated.

Over the years, as one or another wave of xenophobia or unemployment swept over the country, state statutes excluded noncitizens from various callings, employments, and activities: optometrist, dentist, doctor, nurse, architect, teacher, lawyer, policeman, engineer, corporate officer, real estate broker, public accountant, mortician, physiotherapist, pharmacist, pedlar, pool or gambling-hall operator, all or some government or public works employment, hunting, and receiving public charity. It is doubtful that all such statutes have been rigorously enforced, but just before and after the First World War the Supreme Court did uphold a few.[21] In 1915, for example, the Court upheld a New York statute that forbade employment of aliens in public works, in this case the building of the New York City subways. So much, apparently, for the myth that Irish and Italian immigrants built the subways, although I rather think the myth is no myth and that alien labor was widely used. Tammany, bless its memory, surely found a way. In 1923, the Court upheld the most traditional type of alien disability: California and Washington state statutes forbidding aliens to own land; the Court had the Japanese in mind.[22] And as late as 1927 the Court held constitutional a Cincinnati ordinance that limited the issuance of pool-hall licenses to citizens.[23]

In a far more influential decision, *Truax* v. *Raich*, the Court held unconstitutional an Arizona statute imposing a general maximum 20 percent quota on alien employment by private industry (any work-force of more than five employees): the equal protection clause, it said, guaranteed aliens the unrestricted right to earn a living in the common callings.[24] The decision is the authentic voice of the American Constitution, and the Supreme Court in 1971, while holding unconstitutional Arizona and Pennsylvania statutes that attempted to deny welfare benefits to aliens,

21. See, e.g., Heim v. McCall, 239 U.S. 175 (1915) (laborers in public works project); Crane v. New York, 239 U.S. 195 (1915); cf. Patsone v. Pennsylvania, 232 U.S. 138 (1914) (upholding statute forbidding aliens from killing wild game).

22. Frick v. Webb, 263 U.S. 326 (1923); Terrace v. Thompson, 263 U.S. 197 (1923); Porterfield v. Webb, 263 U.S. 225 (1923); Webb v. O'Brien, 263 U.S. 313 (1923).

23. Clarke v. Deckebach, 274 U.S. 392 (1927).

24. Truax v. Raich, 239 U.S. 33 (1915). See also Takahashi v. Fish and Game Commission, 334 U.S. 410 (1948).

went out of its way to emphasize that it is persons, not only citizens, to whom the equal protection clause applies.[25]

That is not quite an end of the matter. Resident aliens are under the protection of our Constitution substantially no less than citizens, but conditions may be attached to entry permits, and in time of war even resident enemy aliens may be subject to fairly harsh restrictions. But that is a consequence, I suggest, of our perception of the meaning of foreign citizenship and of the obligations it may impose more than it is a consequence of the significance of the status of citizen in our own domestic law. The irreducible legal significance more than domestic, and domestic as a reflection of international. The citizen has a right as against the whole world to be here. The alien does not, although once the alien is permanently resident his right to remain, if qualified, is substantial and covered by constitutional protections.[26] The decision of who may enter and remain as of right must be made by every nation-state in a world of nation-states, else it places its existence at risk. Citizenship can be and is made, though rarely, the basis for the extraterritorial application of domestic law (such as the draft, the tax law, rules requiring appearance in court) and, most significantly, for the extraterritorial reach of the quintessential crime of allegiance, the crime of treason, which is defined by the Constitution closely and narrowly in terms of persons, not citizens.[27]

When aroused by the prospect of a railroad strike in 1917 on the eve of war, Justice Holmes said: "Patriotism is the demand of the territorial club for priority, and as much priority as it needs for vital purposes, over such tribal groups as the churches and trade unions. I go the whole hog for the territorial club—and I don't care a damn if it interferes with some of the spontaneities of the other groups."[28] No doubt the territorial club has considerable power to impose its priorities, certainly in time of war, but Holmes

25. Graham v. Richardson, 403 U.S. 365, 371 (1971).
26. See Kwong Hai Chew v. Colding, 344 U.S. 590 (1953).
27. See Kawakita v. United States, 343 U.S. 717 (1952).
28. Oliver W. Holmes to Felix Frankfurter, March 27, 1917, *Holmes Papers* (Harvard Law Library, Cambridge, Mass.).

speaks of the territorial club, not of any construct less physical such as citizenship, and a consequent duty of allegiance. And the territorial club imposes obligations regardless of citizenship: the duty to serve in the armed services by conscription, for example. We draft aliens.

Congress could impose special obligations of allegiance on the citizen but Congress has seldom exerted itself so, and on the rare occasions when it has, it has met resistance from the courts, even to the point of a denial of power to require an oath of allegiance for issuance of a passport.[29]

The naturalization law has long provided that the prospective citizen must be "attached to the principles of the Constitution of the United States and well disposed to the good order and happiness of the United States." But in 1943 the Supreme Court held that an admitted Communist, who had a leadership position in the party, and believed in the dictatorship of the proletariat, though somewhat disingenuously defined, could become a citizen.[30] Attachment to the principles of the Constitution, the Court said, did not mean attachment to any particular principle such as the general form of government, or any particular political philosophy that informs the Constitution, let alone notions of private property. It was sufficient that the applicant was law-abiding, that is, that he did not advocate the violent overthrow of the government, although he assuredly advocated its overthrow.

Chief Justice Harlan F. Stone, dissenting, argued that the Constitution did embody principles and that Congress may require allegiance to them from prospective citizens. Among such principles, Stone said, are "protection of civil rights and of life, liberty and property, the principle of representative government, and the principle that constitutional laws are not to be broken down by planned disobedience."[31] The Constitution was hostile to dictatorship and minority rule, he said, and provided quite plainly the means for its own modification: "It can hardly satisfy the re-

29. Woodward v. Rogers, 344 F. Supp. 974 (D.D.C. 1972); cf. Cole v. Richardson, 405 U.S. 676 (1972).
30. Schneiderman v. United States, 320 U.S. 118 (1943).
31. Ibid. at 181.

quirement of 'attachment to the principles of the Constitution,' that one is attached to the means for its destruction." But that was a minority view, and the majority, despite the surface paradox, held that the principles of the Constitution have to do with people and do not establish some special relationship between an individual who is called a citizen and his government.[32]

In the 1920s the Court had denied naturalization to a pacifist, Rosika Schwimmer, who went with Henry Ford on his peace ship in 1916, and also to an applicant who reserved a right of selective conscientious objection to war, a Professor Macintosh of the Yale Divinity School. But these decisions are not authoritative either; powerful dissents by Charles Evans Hughes, Holmes, Brandeis, and Stone have prevailed to become the accepted law.[33] Special qualifications for naturalization do exist and are enforced. Good moral character is one. However, qualifications that seek to pour ideological and political meaning into the concept of citizenship meet with judicial resistance. Nor has Congress been permitted to define the allegiance of those already citizens by providing for their involuntary expatriation—the involuntary loss of citizenship—upon commission of acts inconsistent with allegiance. Such acts by citizens and even by noncitizens may be punished, but loss of citizenship cannot be predicated on them. And the irony is that in the decisions that denied a power to impose involuntary expatriation and thus seemed to follow the tradition of denuding the concept of citizenship in our law of any special role and content, the Supreme Court returned to a rhetoric of exalting citizenship which echoes the Taney opinion in *Dred Scott.*

In the early years of the Republic, Hamilton and his followers believed that, like British subjects, Americans should be tied

32. There is a later, lower-court case involving a Nazi, which looks the other way, showing perhaps that, in the 1940s anyway, Nazis were thought to be worse than Communists, but it is not an authoritative case. Sittler v. United States, 316 F. 2d 312 (2d Cir. 1963).

33. United States v. Macintosh, 283 U.S. 605 (1931); United States v. Schwimmer, 279 U.S. 644 (1929). See also Girouard v. United States, 328 U.S. 61 (1946).

indissolubly to the state; a right of voluntary expatriation would encourage subversion. But voluntary expatriation has long been permitted by our law. Jefferson supported such a right, and in the end his view prevailed. In 1868 Congress, having for the first time defined citizenship, passed a statute still on the books providing, in warm language, that "the right of expatriation is a natural and inherent right of all people, indispensable to the enjoyment of the rights of life, liberty and the pursuit of happiness," and was not to be denied. We had, after all, fought in 1812 against British claims that immigrants from Great Britain who were sailors in our navy could be treated by the British as deserters because they had never lost their British nationality, and in the 1860s we were indignant at British treatment of naturalized Irish-Americans arrested in Ireland for participation in anti-British activities.[34]

Congress listed as expatriating behavior such acts as voting in a foreign political election or deserting from the armed forces in time of war, or, for a naturalized citizen, taking up permanent residence in the country of his or her birth. In the end the Court held them all unconstitutional,[35] although there is some slight evidence that the Court as now constituted might be willing to some extent to rethink the whole question.[36] The Court said, in effect, in these cases holding the involuntary expatriation statutes unconstitutional, that Congress may not put that much content into the concept of citizenship. It seemed to reaffirm the traditional minimal content of the concept of citizenship, the minimal definition of allegiance. But its language was at war with its action. "This government was born of its citizens," wrote Chief Justice Earl Warren,

> it maintains itself in a continuing relationship with them, and, in my judgment, it is without power to sever the rela-

34. See Charles Gordon, "The Citizen and the State: Power of Congress to Expatriate American Citizens," 53 *Georgetown Law Journal* 315 (1965).

35. Afroyim v. Rusk, 387 U.S. 253 (1967); Schneider v. Rusk, 377 U.S. 163 (1964).

36. See Rogers v. Bellei, 401 U.S. 815 (1971).

tionship that gives rise to its existence. I cannot believe that a government conceived in the spirit of ours was established with power to take from the people their most basic right.

Citizenship *is* man's basic right for it is nothing less than the right to have rights. Remove this priceless possession and there remains a stateless person, disgraced and degraded in the eyes of his countrymen. He has no lawful claim to protection from any nation, and no nation may assert rights on his behalf. His very existence is at the sufferance of the state within whose borders he happens to be. [As if our government were in the habit of beheading people for not being citizens!] In this country the expatriate would presumably enjoy, at most, only the limited rights and privileges of aliens. . . .

The people who created this government endowed it with broad powers. . . . But the citizens themselves are sovereign, and their citizenship is not subject to the general powers of their government.[37]

Citizenship, Warren concluded, is "that status, which alone assures the full enjoyment of the precious rights conferred by our Constitution." Ten years later, when these views came to command a majority,[38] Justice Black wrote: "In our country the people are sovereign and the Government cannot sever its relationship to the people by taking away their citizenship."[39] And: "Its citizenry is the country and the country is its citizenry."[40]

---

37. Perez v. Brownell, 356 U.S. 44, 64–65 (1957) (footnotes omitted) (Warren, Black, and Douglas dissenting). This dissent within the decade became the prevailing view. The chief justice took his clue from an unguarded comment by Brandeis, made in a quite different context, to the effect that deportation of one who claims to be a citizen may result in the loss of "all that makes life worth living." Ng Fung Ho v. White, 259 U.S. 276, 284 (1922).

38. Afroyim v. Rusk, 387 U.S. 253 (1967).

39. Ibid. at 257.

40. Ibid. at 268.

All this, as we have seen, is simply not so. It is not so on the face of the Constitution, and it certainly has not been so since the *Slaughter-House Cases* of 1873. The Warren language was a regression to the confusions of Bingham and, what is worse, to the majority opinion in *Dred Scott* v. *Sandford*, which held that the terms "people of the United States" and "citizens" are synonymous and that they "both describe the political body who according to our republican institutions form the sovereignty." Who said, "They are what we familiarly call the single 'sovereign people,' and every citizen is one of this people and a constituent member of the sovereignty"? Roger B. Taney did, and Earl Warren and Hugo L. Black echoed it a century later, unwittingly to be sure. Who said that noncitizens "had no rights or privileges but such as those who held the power and the government might choose to grant them"? Roger B. Taney, to the same curious later echo.

No matter to what purpose it is put and by whom, this is regressive. Its thrust is parochial and exclusive. A relationship between government and the governed that turns on citizenship can always be dissolved or denied. Citizenship is a legal construct, an abstraction, a theory. No matter what the safeguards, it is at best something given, and given to some and not to others, and it can be taken away. It has always been easier, it always will be easier, to think of someone as a noncitizen than to decide that he is a nonperson, which is the point of the *Dred Scott* case. Emphasis on citizenship as the tie that binds the individual to government and as the source of his rights leads to metaphysical thinking about politics and law, and more particularly to symmetrical thinking, to a search for reciprocity and symmetry and clarity of uncompromised rights and obligations, rationally ranged one next and against the other. Such thinking bodes ill for the endurance of free, flexible, responsive, and stable institutions and of a balance between order and liberty. It is by such thinking, as in Rousseau's *The Social Contract*, that the claims of liberty may be readily translated into the postulates of oppression. I find it gratifying, therefore, that we live under a Constitution to which the concept of citizenship matters very little, that prescribes decencies and wise modalities of government quite without regard to the concept of citizenship. It subsumes important obligations and functions of the individual which have other sources—moral, political, and traditional—sources more complex than the simple contractarian notion of citizenship. "The simple governments," wrote Burke, "are fundamentally defective, to say no worse of them." Citizenship is at best a simple idea for a simple government.

3

Domesticated Civil Disobedience: The First Amendment, from *Sullivan* to the Pentagon Papers

3

Domesticated Civil Disobedience: The First Amendment, from *Sullivan* to the Pentagon Papers

The rights which the First Amendment creates cannot be established by any theoretical definition, as Burke said of the rights of man, but are in "balance between differences of good, in compromises sometimes between good and evil, and sometimes between evil and evil." The computing principle is necessary here, too. The First Amendment is no coherent theory that points our way to unambiguous decisions but a series of compromises and accommodations confronting us again and again with hard questions to which there is no certain answer.

The First Amendment decisions of the Supreme Court, in part, incorporate a "right to disobey," a right that has been controlled and stylized. The amendment makes allowance for domesticated civil disobedience much after the fashion of exemptions for conscientious objection. When, in 1964, the Supreme Court decided *New York Times Company* v. *Sullivan*,[1] the Court, among other things, declared the Sedition Act of 1798 unconstitutional, more than a century and a half after its expiration. Justice delayed, but not denied. The *Sullivan* case was an important and novel decision of great consequence in the law of the First Amendment. In its decision, the Court reversed a judgment in a libel action granted by the Alabama courts to the police commissioner of Montgomery against the *New York Times*. The

1. 376 U.S. 255 (1964).

Times had printed some inaccurate statements about the commissioner in a fund-raising advertisement for Dr. Martin Luther King, Jr., who in turn had run afoul of the commissioner in the course of demonstrations. The Court held that the First Amendment prevents a public official from recovering damages for a defamatory falsehood relating to his official conduct unless he proves that the false statement about him was made with actual knowledge that it was false, or with reckless disregard of whether it was false or not; in other words, with malice. Such a rule, historically quite a new departure, was necessary, the Court said, in order to carry out "a profound national commitment to the principle that debate on public issues should be uninhibited, robust, and wide-open," and that debate should be allowed to include even "vehement, caustic, and sometimes unpleasantly sharp attacks on government and public officials."[2] In the same vein, the Court said in *Rosenbloom* v. *Metromedia, Inc.*,[3] that "freedom of expression, if it would fulfill its historic function in this nation, must embrace all issues about which information is needed or appropriate to enable the members of society to cope with the exigencies of their period." This is as good a statement as any of the public interest the First Amendment seeks to protect.

To require that debate, however uninhibited, robust, wide-open, vehement, caustic, and unpleasantly sharp, be truthful in its factual assertions would certainly dampen the vigor and limit the variety of public debate. It would deprive First Amendment rights, said Justice William J. Brennan for the Court, of necessary breathing space. Would-be critics of official conduct, knowing that they might have to prove their assertions to a jury, might be deterred from making assertions they fully believed to be true. We all know that few statements, however true, can be proved to a mathematical certainty; juries exercise judgment, which is fallible and may be prejudiced, and in any event trials

2. 376 U.S. at 270.
3. 403 U.S. 29 (1971), quoting from Thornhill v. Alabama, 310 U.S. 88, 102 (1940).

are fearfully expensive. As a litigant, Judge Learned Hand once said, "I should dread a lawsuit beyond almost anything else short of sickness and death."[4] The lesson of *New York Times Company* v. *Sullivan*—that the First Amendment guarantees the right to publish falsehood—was well-learned by a Republican Congressman who voted in the summer of 1971, rightly in my judgment, against a resolution that would have cited President Frank Stanton of the Columbia Broadcasting System for contempt of Congress for refusing to make available to Congress editorial matter used in connection with a broadcast called "The Selling of the Pentagon." "The First Amendment," said the Congressman, perhaps unfairly but with acute appreciation of the constitutional position, "guarantees C.B.S. the right to lie, and they exercise it frequently."

The date of the decision in *New York Times Company* v. *Sullivan* is as interesting as its substance. To borrow the Court's phrase, only of late has the First Amendment played, as in *Sullivan*, an "uninhibited, robust, and wide-open" role in our law. Because the First Amendment has been in the Constitution and has had pride of place in the Bill of Rights since 1791, what we may think of as its admonitory career is quite long. But its legal career in court decisions is a matter, essentially, of the past half century. In England and in the colonies in the eighteenth century, and in the United States in the administration of President John Adams, there was a great deal of turmoil and of legal maneuvering about freedom of speech, and more particularly of the press. This was the background and the earliest environment of the First Amendment. But in England, and the more so in the United States, an easy and uncontested freedom of speech and of the press prevailed through the nineteenth century. During this period the First Amendment was legally an unquestioned assumption.

I have no wish to romanticize the nineteenth century. In various localities, especially around the critical contradiction of

4. Association of the Bar of the City of New York, *Lectures on Legal Topics* (New York: Macmillan Co., 1926), 3:105.

slavery, infringements of freedom of speech occurred. Abolitionist speakers were sometimes dealt with harshly by law in the
South and in parts of Northern and Border states. And mobs and
other private forces, abetted from time to time in informal fashion
by public force, imposed their own episodic constraints, sometimes violently. So did one or another military commander in the
Civil War and Reconstruction periods. But there were no systemic, and certainly no nationwide, legal constraints.

Government during the nineteenth century was very far from
the ubiquitous presence that it is now. The late Zechariah Chafee, Jr., the first great scholar of the First Amendment, tells us
that "the [then] prevailing doctrine of *laissez faire* was extended
to the field of discussion. The outstanding representative of the
liberty of the time was John Stuart Mill." It seemed "odd" to
Chafee "to link together the legal restrictions on business and
wealth enacted by collectivists at the opening of the 20th century
and the Sedition laws enacted against collectivists" just about con-
temporaneously, after the long century of consensus and freedom.
Yet Chafee recognized the common impulse behind the social
and economic legislation and the restrictions on freedom of
speech, both of which were ushered in during the twentieth century. The impulse proceeded from social unrest. The movement
for industrial justice disturbed consensus and gave rise to government action regulating industry, on the one hand, and constricting
freedom of speech and of the press on the other. Then followed
judicial decisions testing the reach of the First Amendment. Chafee thought it unfortunate that during the nineteenth century,
"freedom of speech was a cherished tradition, but remained without specific [legal] content."[5] In this we may consider Chafee
mistaken. For law can never make us as secure as we are when
we do not need it. Those freedoms which are neither challenged
nor defined are the most secure. In this sense, for example, it is
true that the American press was freer before it won its battle
with the government in *New York Times Company* v. *United*

5. Zechariah Chafee, *Free Speech in the United States* (Cambridge:
Harvard University Press, 1971), pp. 506–9.

States (Pentagon Papers case) in 1971 than after its victory.[6] Before June 15, 1971, through the troubles of 1798, through one civil and two world wars and other wars, there had never been an effort by the federal government to censor a newspaper by attempting to impose a restraint prior to publication, directly or in litigation. The *New York Times* won its case, over the Pentagon Papers, but that spell was broken, and in a sense freedom was thus diminished.

Prior restraints fall on speech with a brutality and a finality all their own. Even if they are ultimately lifted they cause irremediable loss—a loss in the immediacy, the impact, of speech. They differ from the imposition of criminal liability in significant procedural respects as well, which in turn have their substantive consequences. The violator of a prior restraint may be assured of being held in contempt; the violator of a statute punishing speech criminally knows that he will go before a jury, and may be willing to take his chance, counting on a possible acquittal. A prior restraint, therefore, stops more speech more effectively. A criminal statute chills, prior restraint freezes. Indeed it is the hypothesis of the First Amendment that injury is inflicted on our society when we stifle the immediacy of speech.

But freedom was also extended in the Pentagon Papers case in that the conditions in which government will not be allowed to restrain publication are now clearer and perhaps more stringent than they have been. We are, or at least we feel, freer when we feel no need to extend our freedom. The conflict and contention by which we extend freedom seem to mark, or at least to threaten, a contraction; and in truth they do, for they endanger an assumed freedom which appeared limitless because its limits were untried. Appearance and reality are nearly one. We extend the legal reality of freedom at some cost in its limitless appearance. And the cost is real.

Chafee held that the First Amendment "protects two kinds of

6. The author was chief counsel for the petitioner, The New York Times Company, in the Pentagon Papers case, New York Times Company v. United States, 403 U.S. 713 (1971).

interest in speech. There is an individual interest, the need of many men to express their opinions on matters vital to them if life is to be worth living. . . ." Secondly, Chafee wrote, there is "a social interest in the attainment of truth, so that the country may not only adopt the wisest course of action but carry it out in the wisest way."[7] Now, the interest in truth of which Chafee spoke is not inconsistent with the First Amendment's protection of demonstrable falsehood for, as I have indicated, men may be deterred from speaking what they believe to be true because they fear that it will be found to be false, or that the proof of its truth will be too expensive. Moreover, the individual interest that Chafee mentioned has its truth-seeking aspect. Yet the First Amendment does not operate solely or even chiefly to foster the quest for truth, unless we take the view that truth is entirely a product of the marketplace and is definable as the perceptions of the majority of men, and not otherwise. The social interest that the First Amendment vindicates is rather, as Alexander Meiklejohn[8] and Robert Bork[9] have emphasized, the interest in the successful operation of the political process, so that the country may better be able to adopt the course of action that conforms to the wishes of the greatest number, whether or not it is wise or is founded in truth.

Discussion, the exchange of views, the ventilation of desires and demands—these are crucial to our politics. And so, for much the same reasons, is the effectiveness of the decisions reached by the political process, that is to say, the effectiveness of law embodying the wishes of the greatest number, or at any rate of their chosen representatives. It would follow, then, that the First Amendment should protect and indeed encourage speech so long as it serves to make the political process work, seeking to achieve objectives through the political process by persuading a majority of voters; but *not* when it amounts to

7. Chafee, *Free Speech*, p. 33.
8. See Alexander Meiklejohn, *Free Speech and Its Relation to Self-Government* (New York: Harper and Brothers, 1948).
9. Robert Bork, "Neutral Principles and Some First Amendment Problems," 47 *Indiana Law Journal* 1, 20 et seq. (1971).

an effort to supplant, disrupt, or coerce the process, as by over-throwing the government, by rioting, or by other forms of violence; and also *not* when it constitutes a breach of an otherwise valid law, a violation of majority decisions embodied in law.

There would be considerably less of a problem with the First Amendment if we could distinguish with assurance between speech and conduct, as Justice Black and Justice William O. Douglas sometimes tried to persuade us that we can. Only conduct, their argument has run, can overthrow the government, injure, be violent. Speech cannot. Justice Black's position was that the First Amendment protects only speech, not conduct, and that the protection it extends to speech is absolute. Black would declare with great passion that the text of the First Amendment is, "Congress" —and with the enactment of the Fourteenth Amendment, he believed, this was in effect enlarged to read Congress and the States—"shall make no law . . . abridging the freedom of speech, or of the press." And when the Framers of the Bill of Rights said "no law" they meant "no law." The last words Black spoke from the bench of the Supreme Court during the argument of a case— and throughout his career he had been an active and acute questioner of counsel—came in a question in the Pentagon Papers case,[10] challenging the government to explain how its position could be reconciled with the absolute language of the First Amendment. When Justice Black declared that the Framers who wrote that Congress shall make no law meant no law, Solicitor General Griswold answered: "Now, Mr. Justice, your construction of . . . [the First Amendment] is well known, and I certainly respect it. You say that no law means no law, and that should be obvious. I can only say, Mr. Justice, that to me it is equally obvious that 'no law' does not mean 'no law'. . . ."[11] Very little conduct that involves more than one person is possible without speech. Speech leads to it, merges into it, is necessary to it. That is the point of Justice Holmes's famous metaphor: "The most

10. New York Times Company v. United States, 403 U.S. 713 (1971). Justice Black's comments were made on June 26, 1971 (39 U.S. L.W. 4879).

11. 403 U.S. at 717–18.

stringent protection of free speech would not protect a man in falsely shouting fire in a theater, and causing a panic."[12] It was Holmes also, in the course of a truly fervent defense of free speech, in his dissent in the *Gitlow* case, who said: "Every idea is an incitement. It offers itself for belief and if believed it is acted on unless some other belief outweighs it or some failure of energy stifles the movement at its birth."[13]

There are, then, problems. I have mentioned two. One is the problem of speech which is not discussion informing the political process but which is aimed at dispensing with it, or disrupting it, a coercion of it by violence. Second, there is the problem of speech which is aimed at, or otherwise involves, the violation of a valid law or procedure; speech that has no general purpose of supplanting the political process, but that refuses to accept its operation or its outcome in a given instance. Here I have in mind counseling, or inciting to, disobedience of law—perfectly peaceable disobedience, but disobedience. I have in mind also speech or assembly that involves a breach of laws or procedures which safeguard the public peace and tranquility, or some other public interest; laws or procedures whose validity would not be questioned except as they are violated in the course of engaging in speech or assembly.

That aspect of the first problem—the problem with efforts to supplant or coerce the political process—which is embraced in the historic concept of seditious speech, is dealt with, and perhaps solved as well as may be, by the clear-and-present danger test that Holmes formulated better than half a century ago. The solution is in terms of a judgment, as Holmes often liked to say, of proximity and degree: a pragmatic judgment, drawing a distinction between speech that carried a high risk of disruption, coercion, or violence, and speech that carried no, or less, risk. That judgment is generalized loosely into the clear-and-present-danger formula, under which speech is protected unless it constitutes, in the circumstances, an intentional incitement to

12. Schenck v. United States, 249 U.S. 47, 52 (1919).
13. Gitlow v. New York, 268 U.S. 652, 673 (1925).

imminent forbidden action. Since every idea is an incitement, society would enjoy very little freedom of heated, passionate, or emotional discourse, or altogether of radical discussion, unless Holmes's distinction were drawn and enforced. Shortly before Holmes first formulated the clear-and-present-danger test, Judge Learned Hand wrote: "Detestation of existing policies is easily transformed into forcible resistance of the authority which puts them into execution, and it would be folly to disregard the causal relation between the two. Yet to assimilate agitation . . . with direct incitement to violent resistance is to disregard the tolerance of all methods of political agitation which in normal times is a safeguard of free government."[14] In *Watts* v. *United States,* the Supreme Court dealt with an alleged violation of a statute making it a crime to threaten the life of the president. Watts had said at a public rally that though he had been classified 1-A, "I am not going. If they ever make me carry a rifle, the first man I want to get is LBJ."[15] The Court held that this was "political hyperbole" rather than intentional incitement, and could not form the basis of a criminal prosecution. Political speech, said the Court, is often "vituperative, abusive, inexact."[16] Watts's pronouncement was no more than a crude and offensive statement of opposition to President Johnson.

The clear-and-present-danger test as originally formulated by Holmes also purported to solve the second of the problems I have mentioned—the problem of speech which does not incite to violence or any other coercion of the political process, but merely to the violation of an otherwise valid law or procedure. Our political process, however, is too dependent on registering majority wish, and also intensity of feeling, which it cannot do through the ballot box; it has too many stages of decision-making before laws are ultimately held valid, and too many stages of law-formation which often render law provisional only; and on the other hand it results in a very pervasive government and makes numerous

14. Masses Publishing Co. v. Patten, 244 Fed. 535, 540 (S.D.N.Y. 1917).

15. 394 U.S. 705, 706 (1969).

16. 394 U.S. at 708.

laws and regulations of vastly differing orders of importance. The process is, in sum, too complex, diverse, and resourceful to subsume an unvarying duty to obey all laws. Simple application of the clear-and-present-danger test to forbid all speech which constitutes an intentional incitement to break a law, or all speech which by itself or through its by-products—as in the form of assembly, or of marching, or of handing out leaflets—involves a breach of rules or procedures safeguarding an otherwise valid public interest, would be an anomalous and unrealistic result. It would rest on a snapshot of the political process that showed it as consisting of discussion and voting and nothing else. That is not the whole process, not nearly. It would not work if it were, it would not generate the necessary consent to government, and it would not be stable. We cannot, therefore, as a society, put that kind of store by the duty to obey.

Consequently, quite early, in *Whitney* v. *California*, Brandeis, with Holmes concurring, drew some further distinctions and made occasion for additional judgments of proximity and degree. The fact that speech is likely to result in some violation of law was not enough, he said, to justify its suppression. "There must be the probability of serious injury to the state."[17] And Brandeis gave a very interesting example, calling to mind an ancient and persistent form of civil disobedience: speech that creates an imminent danger of organized trespass on unenclosed, privately owned land. It would be unconstitutional, he suggested, to prohibit such speech, despite the imminent danger it presented, because the harm to society which the prohibition would seek to avert would be "relatively trivial."

Subsequent cases have required government to show not merely a rational, otherwise valid, interest in support of a law or procedure that is endangered or actually violated by speech or by activity attending speech, but a "compelling interest." As the Court said in 1939, in *Schneider* v. *State*,[18] when speech or assembly breaks or threatens to break a law, "the delicate and diffi-

17. 274 U.S. 357, 378 (1927).
18. 308 U.S. 147 (1939).

cult task falls upon the courts to weigh the circumstances and to appraise the substantiality of the reasons advanced in support of" the law in question. Hence, the ultimate formulation of the clear-and-present-danger test, by Judge Hand, is that the courts must ask "whether the gravity of the evil, discounted by its improbability, justifies such invasion of free speech as is necessary to avoid the danger."[19] The nature and gravity of the evil, its gravity as well as its proximity, thus form part of the judicial judgment.

One may ask by what warrant courts decide that some valid laws passed by a legislature are less important than other ones, and may be endangered or disobeyed. The answer is that someone must, unless each and every legitimate but utterly trivial public interest is to prevail over the interest in what Alexander Meiklejohn called "those activities of communication by which we govern."[20] Hence courts do decide. We have thus built into the system a kind of domesticated form of civil disobedience.

It is this aspect of the First Amendment that the Pentagon Papers case of 1971 illustrated and developed, though the case can be viewed in another light, as I shall show. And it had other features. Prior restraints are traditionally disfavored—and in circumstances such as those of the Pentagon Papers publication, with very good reason—even where an attempt might be allowed to regulate the same sort of speech through the *in terrorem* effect of a subsequent sanction. It is unlikely to be held that the First Amendment allows the *in terrorem* effect of criminal prosecution to take away everything that protection against prior restraints is intended to give, and even in some circumstances more. What seems more likely is that the bright line between the one who directly breaches security, at least by leaking if not by stealing, and the one who publishes will be blurred when the courts find themselves confronting both in the same person, as was very nearly true in the case of Daniel Ellsberg and the *Times*. I mean blurred by stretching the protection of the publisher so as to cover the whole transaction. But this is something of a guess, not a

19. Dennis v. United States, 341 U.S. 494 (1951).
20. See Meiklejohn, *Free Speech*.

reading of positive law now in existence. Again, the Pentagon Papers case involved a question of statutory construction and a problem of the separation of powers. Passing over these features, the essence of the government's complaint was that publication of the Pentagon Papers violated a public interest in the confidentiality of government documents, an interest which the executive order establishing the classification system and also, the government contended, the Espionage Act were intended to safeguard. The Espionage Act raised the question of statutory construction to which I have referred, and the attempt to apply the executive order concerning classification of documents—not internally within the executive branch of government, but externally to private persons and entities—gave rise to the problem of separation of powers. Assuming, however, that the government had prevailed on either or both of these points—assuming, that is, acceptance of the government's argument that the public interest in confidentiality of government documents was embodied in valid and applicable law, either in the executive order or in the Espionage Act or both—there remained the issue whether the given injury to this public interest was in the circumstances grave enough to justify a restriction on speech, or too trivial to justify it.

Justice John M. Harlan took the position that the weighing of the gravity of the injury was in this instance not for the judges to undertake, because when the injury is to the nation's foreign relations, as it was plausibly alleged to be, judges should, he thought, simply accept the president's assessment of its gravity. The government did not really contend strongly for this, and no other justice seemed prepared to concede it. Rather, the government tried to persuade the judges themselves that the breach of confidentiality constituted, in the circumstances, a grave and not merely probable, but immediate, injury. The injury was prolongation of the Vietnam war by providing the enemy with helpful information, and embarrassment to the United States in the conduct of diplomatic affairs.

Now, as to the war, there was a question of immediacy, and indeed of causal connection between publication and the feared injury. There was actually nothing more than a tendency, if that, and the bad-tendency test in seditious speech cases is precisely what the clear-and-present-danger doctrine displaced, as its very formulation indicates. It required a high probability instead. As to the claim of embarrassment in the conduct of diplomatic affairs, however, an immediate causal connection was reasonably clear. Here the gravity was squarely in issue. And the court held it insufficient.

The clear-and-present-danger doctrine, then, as it has evolved beyond its original formulation, makes room for what used to be called seditious speech and for a measure of necessary in-system civil disobedience. It gives fair satisfaction, even though it places a bit more reliance in the discretion and prudence of judges than either voluptuaries of liberty or judicial conservatives find altogether comfortable. The underlying, broad principle is that the First Amendment protects the political process and a right of self-expression consistent with its requirements. But other fundamental difficulties remain, which the clear-and-present-danger test rather tends to sweep under the rug. Obviously the political process is not what we pursue everywhere, for purposes of all decision-making, or always. There are times when we do not, and places where we do not, and times when the need for self-expression is also not a dominant interest. Equally obviously, not all the results that the political process might attain are acceptable.

Thus a criminal trial to a jury does not operate on the rules of the political process or as a forum for self-expression, and if a witness, therefore, should wish to recite some hearsay evidence to the jury, we stop him. We forbid him to speak. We might also, and we should, as Justice Black intimated in *Cox* v. *Louisiana*, although in dissent, stop a speaker from assailing a trial by haranguing a crowd on the courthouse lawn while the trial is proceeding. "Government under law as ordained by our Constitution is too precious, too sacred," said Black, "to be jeopardized by subjecting the courts to intimidatory practices that have been fatal to individual liberty and minority rights wherever such practices have been allowed to poison the streams of justice."[21] What

21. 379 U.S. 559, 584 (1965).

is meant by intimidatory practices is public opinion impinging too proximately and too directly on the trial. Only a year later, in 1966, in *Adderly* v. *Florida*,[22] Justice Black, now in the majority, indicated that the grounds of a jail were also no place for free expression of views. The democratic political process is not the method by which we conduct trials, it is not what prevails within a jail or around it, and where it does not prevail, the First Amendment should not protect speech that in other circumstances would be protected. Faculties that just a few years ago felt embarrassed to exclude students from their deliberations might have remembered that. A university is also not governed by the democratic political process. We recognize times when that process is suspended even in places where ordinarily it does rule. Hence curfews, hence martial law.

In approaching the other and greater difficulty—unacceptable results that the political process, with free speech as a principal component, might reach, or unacceptable acts that speech might counsel its hearers to engage in—one wants to be extremely careful not to be understood as following the teaching of Herbert Marcuse. But that does not mean that the problem shouldn't be stated and faced. Take, for example, the advocacy—not the intentional incitement, which the clear-and-present-danger test does allow us to reach—but the advocacy of genocide. Or, to recall what is more familiar, suppose, more minimally, a speech as in *Beauharnais* v. *Illinois*,[23] decided in 1952, which urged the segregation of Negroes on the ground that they are all given to rape, robbery, knives, guns, and marijuana. Or the speech in *Brandenburg* v. *Ohio*,[24] decided in 1969: "I believe the nigger should be returned to Africa, the Jew returned to Israel." Or the speech in a case of the early 1950s *Kunz* v. *New York*:[25] "All the garbage that didn't believe in Christ should have been burnt in the incinerators. It's a shame they all weren't." Or Jerry Rubin, at May Day in New Haven in 1970, urging the young to go home

22. 385 U.S. 39 (1966).
23. 343 U.S. 250 (1952).
24. 395 U.S. 444 (1969).
25. 340 U.S. 290, 296 (1951).

and kill their parents; or other talk looking with favor on murder, rape, fire, and destruction.

Writing in *Kunz* v. *New York*, not long after his experience as prosecutor at the Nuremberg trials, Justice Robert H. Jackson said:

> Essential freedoms are today threatened from without and within. It may become difficult to preserve here what a large part of the world has lost—the right to speak, even temperately, on matters vital to spirit and body. In such a setting, to blanket hateful and hate-stirring attacks on races and faiths under the protections for freedom of speech may be a noble innovation. On the other hand, it may be a quixotic tilt at windmills which belittles great principles of liberty. Only time can tell. But I incline to the latter view.[26]

Leaving aside for the moment the question whether there are greater dangers in trying to define and control the sort of speech I have been reciting than in risking that it will achieve the results it advocates, one may allow such speech on one of two premises: either the cynical premise that words don't matter, that they make nothing happen and are too trivial to bother with; or else the premise taken by Justice Brandeis in *Whitney* v. *California* that "discussion affords ordinarily adequate protection against the dissemination of noxious doctrine."[27]

The first premise is inconsistent with the idea of a First Amendment; if speech doesn't matter we might as well suppress it, because it is sometimes a nuisance. As to the second, we have lived through too much to believe it. To be sure, Justice Brandeis adhered to the clear-and-present-danger test, and conceded, therefore, that in circumstances of emergent danger we can stop speech. But we know, as Brandeis may have allowed himself to forget, that speech can attain unacceptable ends even if it does not have the qualities of incitement, and even if it comes from people who lack the intent to achieve those ends.

26. 340 U.S. 290, 295 (1951).
27. 274 U.S. 357, 375 (1927).

Disastrously, unacceptably noxious doctrine can prevail, and can be made to prevail by the most innocent sort of advocacy. Holmes recognized as much in the passage in the *Gitlow* dissent in which he said that "eloquence may set fire to reason." In the *Gitlow* case itself he saw neither incitement nor eloquence and no chance of a present conflagration, no clear and present danger. Yet he did admit that all ideas carried the seed of future dangers as well as benefits. His answer was this: "If in the long run the beliefs expressed in proletarian dictatorship are destined to be accepted by the dominant forces of the community, the only meaning of free speech [—*the only*—] is that they should be given their chance and have their way."[28] If in the long run the belief, let us say, in genocide is destined to be accepted by the dominant forces of the community, the only meaning of free speech is that it should be given its chance and have its way. Do we believe that? Do we accept it?

Even speech which advocates no idea can have its consequences. It may inflict injury by its very utterance, as the Court said a generation ago, in the *Chaplinsky* case, of lewd or profane or fighting words.[29] There is such a thing as verbal violence, a kind of cursing, assaultive speech that amounts to almost physical aggression, bullying that is no less punishing because it is simulated. Thus there is a difference, although in a 1971 decision the Supreme Court managed not to perceive it, between carrying a sign in public that says, Down with the Draft, and a sign that says—I bowdlerize—Fornicate the Draft;[30] between a publication that vigorously criticizes the police and one that depicts them in a cartoon as raping the Statue of Liberty; between using all manner of epithets and employing a fashionable one which is quaintly abbreviated, "mother."[31] This sort of speech constitutes an assault. More, and equally important, it may create a climate, an environment in which conduct and actions that were not possible before become possible. It is from this point of view

28. 268 U.S. 652, 673 (1925).
29. Chaplinsky v. New Hampshire, 315 U.S. 568 (1942).
30. See Cohen v. California, 403 U.S. 15 (1971).
31. See Papish v. Board of Curators, 464 F. 2d 136 (8th Cir. 1972).

that the decision in the *Watts* case, in which the Court passed off as political hyperbole an expressed intention to shoot the president, is perhaps dubious. We have been listening for years—though the level of it in the universities is happily on the decline—to countless apocalyptic pronouncements and to filthy and violent rhetoric, and have dealt with them as speech, as statements of a position, of one side of an issue, to which we may respond by disagreeing, while necessarily accepting by implication the legitimacy of the statement, the right of the speaker to make it.

To listen to something on the assumption of the speaker's right to say it is to legitimate it. There is a story—I cannot vouch for its accuracy, but I found it plausible—of a crowd gathered in front of the ROTC building at a university some years ago. At this university, as elsewhere, some members of the faculty and administration had undertaken to discharge the function of cardinal legate to the barbarians, going without the walls every so often to negotiate the sack of the city. On this occasion, with the best of intentions, members of the faculty joined the crowd and participated in discussing the question whether or not to set fire to the building. The faculty, I gather, took the negative, and I assume that none of the students arguing the affirmative could have been deemed guilty of inciting the crowd. The matter was ultimately voted upon, and the affirmative lost—narrowly. But the negative taken by the faculty was only one side of a debate which the faculty rendered legitimate by engaging in it. Where nothing is unspeakable, nothing is undoable.

This is also the problem with obscenity. The question about obscenity is not whether books get girls pregnant, or sexy or violent movies turn men to crime. To view it in this way is to try to shoehorn the obscenity problem into the clear-and-present-danger analysis, and the fit is a bad one. Books, let us assume, do not get girls pregnant; at any rate, there are plenty of other efficient causes of pregnancy, as of crime. We may assume further that it is right to protect privacy, and that we have no business, therefore, punishing anyone for amusing himself obscenely in his home. But the question is, should there be a right to obtain obscene books and pictures in the market, or to foregather in public places—discreet, but accessible to all—with others who share a taste for the obscene? To grant this right is to affect the world about the rest of us, and to impinge on other privacies and other interests, as those concerned with the theater in New York have found, apparently to their surprise. Perhaps each of us can, if he wishes, effectively avert the eye and stop the ear. Still, what is commonly read and seen and heard and done intrudes upon us all, wanted or not, for it constitutes our environment.

The problem is no different from that raised by the physical environment, or by indecent exposure, by boisterous drunkenness, rampant prostitution, or public lovemaking. Yet each of us cannot but tolerate a very great deal that violates our freedom and privacy in these senses, because the alternative is to let government, acting perhaps in behalf of a majority, control it all; and that is tyranny—massive tyranny, if it works, selective or occasional and random tyranny if, as is more likely, it does not work very well. Yet the same Supreme Court which decreed virtually unlimited permissiveness with regard to obscenity has not construed the Constitution so as to forbid the placing of legal restraints on architectural designs, for example, or on indecencies of public behavior. Nor is the Court very likely to tell us that fostering heterosexual marriage while not countenancing homosexual unions, which is what the legal order does, of course, is unconstitutional. The assigned reason is that the First Amendment throws special safeguards around speech and other forms of communication, which are relevant to obscenity, but does not protect conduct. The point is absurd. There is no bright line between communication and conduct. What is a live sex show—communication or conduct?

Law which attempts to come to grips with the problem of obscenity—or aesthetics in the physical environment, or drinking, or exposure of the body, or drug-taking, or offensive or assaultive speech—is a subtler kind of instrument, running greater risks and expecting to attain a rather more remote approximation of its ends than the law which forbids murder and theft, or defines the rights and obligations of a property-owner, or governs the relations between General Motors and the United Automobile Work-

ers of America. Very little of what is called law achieves its ends
always or precisely. But much of it tries to, because it is fully
confident of the validity of its ends, which it can and does define
intelligibly and with some precision. A law attempting to regulate obscenity, however, has to exist in a peculiar tension. It must
avoid tyrannical enforcement of supposed majority tastes, while
providing visible support for the diffuse private endeavors of an
overwhelming majority of people to sustain the style and quality
of life minimally congenial to them. This sort of law necessarily
accepts a certain ambiguity about its ends. Even the mere effort to
enforce such a law perfectly, or with the intent to achieve the
nearest possible approximation of perfection, as the law against
murder is enforced—even this effort would verge in practice on
the tyrannical. And if the life style of large numbers of people
changes despite the law, or cannot successfully be affected by it,
so that any sort of even-handed enforcement at all, however
minimal, is impossible, then any enforcement becomes tyrannical
and the law must be abandoned, as we abandoned prohibition
of liquor and ought perhaps to abandon prohibition of marijuana.
Again, if such a law, even though vigorously enforced, turns out
hardly to touch the activity it forbids, because the motive to engage in it is too strong, then all the law achieves by making the
activity illegal is to place an economic tariff on it and to cause
a "ripple effect" of crime. This, as Professor Herbert L. Packer
pointed out,[32] is the case with laws that punish gambling or the
taking of addictive drugs. These laws ought to be repealed and
replaced by other forms of regulation that are less productive of
undesirable side effects.

The short of it is that its very existence, and occasional but
steady enforcement in aggravated cases for the sake of making itself visible, is the real and virtually sole purpose of a law against
obscenity. Its role is supportive, tentative, even provisional. It
walks a tightrope, and runs high risks. On occasion, in some cor-
ner of the country, some fool finds Chaucer obscene or the lower

32. Herbert L. Packer, *The Limits of the Criminal Sanction* (Stanford;
Stanford University Press, 1968), pp. 277 et seq.

female leg indecent. For this reason the federal government itself, as Justice Harlan has long argued and as Chief Justice Warren Burger has agreed, should stay out of the business of censorship altogether, because its idiocies, when they occur, affect the whole country.[33] But the Supreme Court, while exercising procedural oversight, ought to let state and local governments run the risks if they wish. For the stakes are high.

I state these problems without having a general solution to offer. They are uninhibited, robust, and intractable, although so far as obscenity, at least, is concerned, the Supreme Court could well have permitted some inhibitions of the more robust forms of it without needing to confront the ultimately intractable dilemma I shall pose. The argument for resolving these problems by extending protection to speech—except as the clear-and-present-danger formula would limit—is stated by Holmes in the dissent in *Abrams* v. *New York*:[34] "Persecution for the expression of opinions seems to me perfectly logical. If you have no doubt of your premises or your power and want a certain result with all your heart you naturally express your wishes in law and sweep away all opposition." To allow opposition by speech, Holmes continues, indicates either that you think the speech does not matter, or that you doubt your power or your premises. He goes on:

> But when men have realized that time has upset many fighting faiths, they may come to believe even more than they believe the very foundations of their own conduct that the ultimate good desired is better reached by free trade in ideas—that the best test of truth is the power of the thought to get itself accepted in the competition of the market, and that truth is the only ground upon which their wishes safely can be carried out.

This is the point at which one asks whether the best test of the idea of proletarian dictatorship, or segregation, or genocide is

33. See Stanley v. Georgia, 394 U.S. 557 (1969).
34. Abrams v. New York, 250 U.S. 616, 630 (1919).

really the marketplace, whether our experience has not taught us that even such ideas can get themselves accepted there, and that a marketplace without rules of civil discourse is no marketplace of ideas, but a bullring.

The theory of the truth of the marketplace, Holmes concluded, expressing more his own view than that of the Philadelphia Convention, "is the theory of our Constitution. It is an experiment, as all life is an experiment." But the theory of the truth of the marketplace, determined ultimately by a count of noses—this total relativism—cannot be the theory of our Constitution, or there would be no Bill of Rights in it, and certainly no Supreme Court to enforce it. It amused Holmes to pretend that if his fellow citizens wanted to go to hell in a basket he would help them. It was his job, he said. Sometimes he did, to be sure, and sometimes it was his job as judge. But not his sole job, and not always. And Holmes knew that, too. He had what he called his "can't helps," and he knew that the Framers of the Constitution had had theirs, and somewhere in the combination of his "can't helps"— of the Framers', of his fellow judges', and of those of other leaders of opinion—were to be found the values of the society. If his fellow citizens wanted to consign these values to hell, perhaps they could do so, but it was not Holmes's job to help them.

"I do not know what is true," said Holmes. "I do not know the meaning of the universe." His biographer, Mark DeWolfe Howe, wondered whether our stomachs were "strong enough to accept the bitter pill which Holmes tendered us." They had better be. We had better recognize how much is human activity a random confusion, and that there is no final validity to be claimed for our truths. If we allow ourselves to be engulfed in moral certitudes we will march to self-destruction from one Vietnam and one domestic revolution—sometimes Marcusean and often not— to another. And yet we do need, individually and as a society, some values, some belief in the foundations of our conduct, in order to make life bearable. If these too are lies, they are, as Holmes's great contemporary, Joseph Conrad, thought them, true lies; if illusions, then indispensable ones. To abandon them is to commit moral suicide.

Whom are we to trust as the custodians and enforcers of those few beliefs which constitute the foundations of our conduct? Passing majorities of the moment? That is the marketplace, which the First Amendment may enjoin us to guard, but not to trust, certainly not to trust to govern access to itself. Whom then? Electorally irresponsible courts? It is one thing to rely on them to keep the marketplace open, another to permit them to close it, even though we do trust our courts to guard some values against majoritarian subversion. We have no answer to these questions, and that is the real reason why we prefer, so often, to err on the side of permissiveness. But we should know also that we err—on the right side, perhaps, but we err.

Actually, ambiguity and ambivalence, not the theory of the truth of the marketplace as Holmes would have had us think, is, if not the theory, at any rate the condition, of the First Amendment in the law of our Constitution. Nothing is more characteristic of the law of the First Amendment—not the rhetoric, but the actual law of it—than the Supreme Court's resourceful efforts to cushion rather than resolve clashes between the First Amendment and interests conflicting with it. The Court's chief concern has been with procedural compromises (using the term in a large sense), and with accommodations that rely on the separation and diffusion of power. A great deal of freedom of speech can flourish in a democratic society which naturally shares, or accepts from its judges or other pastors, a minimal definition of the good, the beautiful, the true, and the properly civil. A great deal of freedom of speech can flourish as well, for a time at any rate, in a society which accepts the proposition of bullring, or marketplace, truth. We are neither society. We have tended to resemble the latter, of late, and we have more freedom than the former might enjoy, and than we enjoyed in the nineteenth century, but we are actually more nearly the former. Freedom of speech, with us, is a compromise, an accommodation. There is nothing else it could be.

The devices of compromise and accommodation that are perhaps in commonest use go by the names of vagueness and overbreadth. The Court will not accept infringements on free speech by administrative or executive action, and if the infringement occurs pursuant to a statute, the Court will demand that the statute express the wish of the legislature in the clearest, most precise, and narrowest fashion possible. Essentially what the Court is exacting is assurance that the judgment that speech should be suppressed is made by the full, pluralist, open political process, not by someone down the line, representing only one or another particular segment of the society; and assurance that the judgment has been made closely and deliberately, with awareness of the consequences and with clear focus on the sort of speech the legislature wished to suppress.

An accommodation relying on the diffusion and separation of powers is what the Pentagon Papers case amounted to in the end. Not long after the case was decided, in September 1971, the president invoked what is called executive privilege to deny to the Senate Foreign Relations Committee access to certain documents bearing on long-range plans for foreign military assistance. This was but one of the numerous invocations of executive privilege on the part of Nixon and previous presidents, and whatever the merits of this particular invocation of it, there is little doubt of the president's authority, in general, to safeguard the privacy of executive deliberations by classifying documents and withholding them from Congress, and of course from the public. Yet under the *New York Times* case, if a newspaper had got hold of these documents without itself participating in a theft of them, although somebody else might to its knowledge have stolen them, it could have published them with impunity. And if someone stole these documents and brought them to a senator, he could use them and read them on the floor of the Senate if he chose, thus making them public, and there would be no recourse against him because of the immunity the Constitution grants to members of Congress in respect of statements on the floor, or, for that matter, in committee.

This is a paradox to say the least. The government is entitled to keep things private and will attain as much privacy as it can get away with politically by guarding its privacy internally; but with few exceptions involving the highest probability of very

grave consequences, it may not do so effectively. It is severely
limited as to means, being restricted, by and large, to enforcing
security at the source. There are things government may not do,
generally or to guard privacy. It may not spy electronically without a judicial warrant, except perhaps if the subject of its sur-
veillance is a foreign government, and it may not steal, or break
and enter, or commit other ordinary crimes any more than anyone else. Yet the power to arrange security at the source, looked at
in itself, is great, and if it were nowhere countervailed it would
be quite frightening—is anyway, perhaps—since the law in no
wise guarantees its prudent exercise or even effectively guards
against its abuse. But there *is* countervailing power. The press, by
which is meant anybody, not only the institutionalized print and
electronic press, can be prevented from publishing only in extreme and quite dire circumstances. The rule of the Pentagon
Papers case calls for evidence of immediate harm of the gravest
sort (typically loss of life or catastrophic injury to the national
interest) flowing directly and ineluctably from publication, before
a restraint will be allowed. We have no Official Secrets Act and
can have none restraining publication of most secrets. The government cannot copyright anything, and almost certainly has no
common-law literary property rights either. It does not own the
contents of its documents. So government may guard mightily
against serious but more ordinary leaks, and yet must suffer them
if they occur. Members of Congress as well as the press may
publish materials that the government wishes to, and is entitled
to, keep private. It is a disorderly situation surely. But if we
ordered it we would have to sacrifice one of two contending
values—privacy or public discourse—which are ultimately irreconcilable. If we should let the government censor as well as withhold, that would be too much dangerous power, and too much
privacy. If we should allow the government neither to censor
nor to withhold, that would provide for too little privacy of
decision-making and too much power in the press and in
Congress.

The adversary game between press and government is effective, its rules essentially the rules of contest, not governing the

result; they are loose and unenforceable except by each player for himself. But without observance, there is no game. One rule of the game is that government secrecy may not be indiscriminate because, carried far enough, such secrecy will destroy the political process. It is dangerous to rely essentially on the government's self-restraint and self-discipline to keep the drive for secrecy within bounds; but that, as induced and disciplined by the political process itself, and subject to the countervailing function of the press, is all there is. There is nothing courts can do to a runaway president or a runaway Congress which has thrown off all self-discipline. If the president, for example, had kicked over the traces and sent the Marines to retrieve the Pentagon Papers from the *New York Times* there would be nothing to discuss; an exercise of raw power would have taken place, to which the only reply, if any, is equally raw power.

The game similarly calls on the press to consider the responsibilities that its position implies. Not everything is fit to print. There is to be regard for at least probable factual accuracy, for danger to innocent lives, for human decencies, and even, if cautiously, for nonpartisan considerations of the national interest. Here, too, reliance is on self-discipline and self-restraint, and on public opinion, not on law. But I should add that as I conceive the contest established by the First Amendment, and as the Supreme Court of the United States appeared to conceive it in the Pentagon Papers case, the presumptive duty of the press is to publish, not to guard security or to be concerned with the morals of its sources. Those responsibilities rest chiefly elsewhere. Within self-disciplined limits and presumptively, the press is a morally neutral, even an unconcerned, agent as regards the provenance of newsworthy material that comes to hand; and within like limits and again presumptively, the press is not the judge or the definer of the national interest. It is, rather, one party to a contest. Its chief responsibility is to play its role in that contest, for it is the contest that serves the public interest, which is not wholly identified either with the interest of the government of the day, or of the press.

The contest between press and government is in a sense analogous to the collision between prosecutor and defense in our system of the administration of criminal justice. Ours is an adversary, accusatory system, as opposed to the European inquisitorial system. Police and prosecutors, with us, are supposed to seek justice, of course, but we channel their zeal to the pursuit of evidence of guilt, and train them to rely on the defense to find and present to an impartial third party evidence of innocence. We rely on the collision between prosecution and defense to produce the just result. We choose to believe also that men are presumptively innocent and owe the state no duty to prove themselves so. And if they owed any such duty at all they would owe it not to police and prosecutors, but to judge and jury, who alone are deemed impartial. This adversary system may not be the best, the most efficient, or ultimately the most just. But the worst and most unjust system is assuredly a mixed one, an adversary system which weights the scales, contrary to its fundamental premises, in favor of the prosecution.

The game theory of the First Amendment is for me the useful point of entry also into the newsmen's privilege problem, as it is called. The paradox is frequently remarked on that reporters couple an insistence on protection of their confidences with an insistence on access to the confidences of others. The chief justice made the point in a question at the argument of the Pentagon Papers case, months before the newsmen's privilege issue had reached the Supreme Court.[35]

Now, on the surface, the position does appear anomalous. A certain asymmetry, a lack of evenhandedness, a certain partiality to self may be detected in the reporter's position. But there is no insistence on unrestricted access by reporters to others' confidences. And the reporter's position in seeking access will appear self-serving only if the focus is on the reporter's pursuit of his own interest, that is, psychic and material gain from the practice of his profession; and if, in turn, the focus is on the personal interest of the individual to whose confidences the reporter seeks access. If

35. See Abraham Goldstein, "Newsmen and their Confidential Sources," *New Republic* 162 (March 21, 1970), 13–15.

nothing more than this were in play between the reporter and his professional adversaries, there would be some justice in the view that the scales ought to be even. When the focus shifts, as it ought, to the function each performs, the earlier appearance tends to vanish. The interest of the reporter and of his adversaries is joined to the function of each, so that each may perform it with zeal. The reporter seeks access to confidences; the newsmaker seeks control over the news he makes. But the weight of the First Amendment is on the reporter's side, because the assumption underlying the First Amendment is that secrecy and the control of news are all too inviting, all too easily achieved, and, in general, all too undesirable. The First Amendment weds the public interest in the flow of news—a major public interest, no doubt, but in some circumstances not the sole one—to the reporter's professional interest, and it is this public interest, not the reporter's alone, that overrides what might in private relationships seem to be the dictates of fairness and equity. The professional interest of the reporter is, in an apposite phrase of Madison, "a sentinel over the public rights."[36]

Historically the law has recognized no reporter's privilege, although undoubtedly judges and prosecuting officials in informal arrangements have taken the reporter's position into account. And even the most absolutist of literalists and the most literal of absolutists would have to admit that before denial of reporter's privilege can be held to abridge the freedom of the press, some applicable meaning must be reasoned into the phrase "freedom of the press" which does not necessarily leap to the eye upon a mere reading of it. Equally obviously the First Amendment lends itself without a forcing of the language to a recognition of the problem, and I greatly regret that the Supreme Court largely washed its hands of it.[37] To be sure, the Supreme Court's decision took away no previously acknowledged right. The Court was invited to establish in the law of the Constitution a right the press has urged

36. *The Federalist*, No. 51, ed. Jacob Cooke (Middletown, Conn.: Wesleyan University Press, 1961), pp. 347, 349.
37. Branzburg v. Hayes, 408 U.S. 665 (1972).

as necessary, one in practice often extended as a privilege.[38] The Court declined the invitation. But the Court's decision has undoubtedly encouraged prosecutors—state more than federal—to subpoena reporters. Still, there may be some legislative help, and even without it the rash of subpoenas may diminish or even vanish.

The main point goes to the nature and scope of the protection that ought to be claimed. I think it demonstrable that if all confidences a reporter receives as he gathers news are automatically and readily available to government investigators in any and all circumstances, sources of confidential information will dry up, or most of them will, greatly impoverishing public discourse. Indispensable information comes in confidence from officeholders fearful of superiors, from businessmen fearful of competitors, from informers operating at the edge of the law who are in danger of reprisal from criminal associates, from people afraid of the law and of government—sometimes rightly afraid, but as often from an excess of caution—and from men in all fields anxious not to incur censure for unorthodox or unpopular views, whether their views would be considered unorthodox and be unpopular in the community at large, or merely in their own group or subculture. Forcing reporters to divulge such confidences would dam the flow to the press, and through it to the people, of the most valuable sort of information: not the press release, not the handout, but the firsthand story based on the candid talk of a primary news source. Although the direct censorship of newspapers or broadcasts would constitute a more blatant—because historically more familiar and, of course, differently motivated—violation of the First Amendment, the forcing of disclosure of reporters' confidences is not very different in effect. It is a form of indirect, and perhaps random, but highly effective censorship; a prior restraint, not in the sense in which those words are used as a phrase of art, but in a literal and constitutionally also relevant sense. For the

38. The author joined in the invitation in an *amicus* brief he filed for a number of clients.

forced disclosure of reporters' confidences will abort the gathering and analysis of news, and thus, of course, restrain its dissemination. The reporter's access *is* the public's access. He has, as a citizen, his own First Amendment rights to self-expression, to speech and to association activity, but they are not in question here. The issue is the public's right to know. That right is the reporter's by virtue of the proxy which the freedom of the press clause of the First Amendment gives to the press in behalf of the public.

Yet it makes no sense from this premise to urge an all-encompassing, absolute privilege for reporters, a virtual insulation of the press from all government investigations and from the process of administering justice, civil and criminal. It is difficult to justify a reporter's privilege where no confidentiality is involved, where, for example, some news sources refuse to communicate with a reporter even about subject matter neither confidential nor illegal if he cannot credibly promise that under no circumstances would he obey a government subpoena, or be subject to one. It is difficult, in other words, to accept that a reporter's First Amendment protection should be tailored to the whim, to the irrational anxiety, the arbitrary edict, the ideological fixation of one or another news source; difficult to accept such a veto over the reporter in the pursuit of his profession, or the government in the discharge of its responsibility to administer justice. It is difficult to agree, even where confidences are involved, that the rule against violating them must be absolute, no matter what else is in play—a parade of horribles, the safety of a kidnap victim, or the gravest considerations of national security. Obviously the occasions when a reporter will witness a so-called natural crime in confidence, and the occasions when he will find it conformable to his own ethical and moral standards to withhold information about such a crime are bound to be infinitesimally few. It does not strengthen a valid case for the press to claim an absolute privilege and then to say, trust us not to exercise it absolutely. We trust much to benevolent discretion, in public and private sectors, but generally only when countervailed. The government itself lost resoundingly when it claimed an absolute right to wiretap in national security cases, arguing that it would exercise it with moderation.[39]

Neither is the right to publish absolute; nothing is. Private rights, including the right not to be maliciously defamed and a right to literary property, still limit the freedom to print, and so do some public rights. Newspapers have, for example, been enjoined, under the Civil Rights Act of 1968, from printing advertisements for the sale of real estate to whites only; here government action is exerted to attain the government's objective not only by action against the seller, but by pursuit of the publisher. The publisher is said to have a commercial interest in such cases, but he always has, and political opinion is not irrelevant to publication of racially discriminatory advertisements.[40] And an injunction forbidding publication, falling indirectly on the publisher, may be issued to a former government employee when publication would violate the employee's contractual obligation not to publish the government's secrets.[41] So we are content, in the contest between press and government, with the pulling and hauling, because in it lies the optimal assurance of both privacy and freedom of information. Not full assurance of either, but maximum assurance of both.

Madison knew the secret of this disorderly system, indeed he invented it. The secret is the separation and balance of powers, men's ambition joined to the requirements of their office, so that they push those requirements to the limit, which in turn is set by the contrary requirements of another office, joined to the ambition of other men. This is not an arrangement whose justification is efficiency, logic, or clarity. Its justification is that it accommodates power to freedom and vice versa. It reconciles the irreconcilable.

39. United States v. United States District Court, 407 U.S. 297 (1972).
40. United States v. Hunter, 459 F. 2d 205 (4th Cir. 1972); cf. Capital Broadcasting v. Mitchell, 333 F. Supp. 582 (D.D.C. 1971); Pittsburgh Press Co. v. Pittsburgh Commission on Human Relations, 413 U.S. 376 (1973).
41. United States v. Marchetti, 466 F. 2d 1309 (4th Cir. 1972), cert. denied, 409 U.S. 1063 (1972).

Madison's conception of the separation and diffusion of powers was intragovernmental, but the First Amendment, as the Pentagon Papers case demonstrated, extends it beyond government, so that it prevails not only among the institutions of government but also between them and the private sector. The First Amendment offers us no formula describing the degree of freedom of information that is consistent with necessary privacy of government decision-making. Rather, as the Supreme Court applied it, it ordains an unruly contest between the press, whose office is freedom of information and whose ambition is joined to that office, and government, whose need is often the privacy of decision-making and whose servants are ambitious to satisfy that need.

I do not say that we can get along without any restraint or self-discipline on the part of government and the press in the discharge of their respective offices and in the ambitious pursuit by each of its interest. Not at all. But it is the contest that serves the interest of society as a whole, which is identified neither with the interest of the government alone nor of the press. The best resolution of this contest lies in an untidy accommodation; like democracy, in Churchill's aphorism, it is the worst possible solution, except for all the other ones. It leaves too much power in government, and too much in the institutionalized press, too much power insufficiently diffused, indeed all too concentrated, both in government and in too few national press institutions, print and electronic. The accommodation works well only when there is forbearance and continence on both sides. It threatens to break down when the adversaries turn into enemies, when they break diplomatic relations with each other, gird for and wage war. Such conditions threaten graver breakdowns yet, eroding the popular trust and confidence in both government and press on which effective exercise of the function of both depends. Faced with ineluctable, fundamental tensions that are bound to persist, the Court as often as not has attempted to ease rather than finally resolve them. Thus the Court has exacted the strictest, even the extraordinary, observance of legislative, judicial, and administrative procedures, to the end of moderating or avoiding a clash with First Amendment values. The Court has, as occasion offered, devised special procedures tailored to this end. The upshot, happily, is that a whole series of defensive procedural entrenchments lie between the First Amendment and interests adverse to it. Hence the direct, ultimate confrontation is rare and when it does occur, limited and manageable. We thus contrive to avoid most judgments that we do not know how to make.

There are no absolutes that a complex society can live with in its law. There is only the computing principle that Burke spoke of—adding, subtracting, multiplying, dividing. A very broad freedom to print, and a very considerable freedom to ferret out information by all manner of means ought to be, and substantially has been, one of the chief denominations computed in our calculus as constitutional policy. But there are other denominations as well. It is the most enduring instinct of our legal order, which is more Burkean than some care to acknowledge, to resist the assertion of absolute claims and, therefore, a waste of breath to make them. Even absolute rights that the legal order seems, absentmindedly, to create, if very rarely, do not endure. Circumstances erode them. Better to recognize from the first that the computing principle is all there is, ought to be, or can be.

4

Civil Disobedience, Revolution, and the Legal Order

4

Civil Disobedience, Revolution, and the Legal Order

Civil Disobedience and the
Limits of Law

Some time ago, before the magnitude of the scandals of the Nixon administration was perceived, there was some self-serving talk of a commonality of error among the Watergate perpetrators, as the arresting officers might have called them, and the radical Left of the 1960s. Too much zeal, that had been the sin of his people, President Nixon himself suggested in one of his Watergate speeches in the spring of 1973; it was a sin and inexcusable, but also venial. Like the zealots of the Left, his people had put their cause above the law. But they had been led into their error by the toleration that much liberal opinion had shown for the zealotry of the Left, for the draft-dodgers and demonstrators of all sorts. The lesson to be drawn was that the law is sacred, rising above all causes, and no violation of it is excusable, none. A rededication to law and order on all sides, by all factions, was called for. Indeed, Mr. Nixon had long been calling for it. Watergate, we were left to infer, was actually a vindication of the president's long-held position, and a reproach to that large body of liberal opinion which had tolerated lawlessness, and ended by infecting even the righteous with it.

The point was most vividly if plaintively called to attention by Jeb Stuart Magruder, who reminded us that he had been taught ethics at Williams College by William Sloane Coffin, Jr. The symbolic expression of the theme! This was all a vulgar attempt to exonerate the dishonorable, a prelude to plea-bargaining. And yet, to use the idiom of the Watergate actors, there is a point of contact. I don't know how many of Mr. Nixon's men can be credited, if that is the word, with self-righteous moral or ideological motivation. But perhaps for some of them moral or ideological imperatives clashed with the legal order more or less as they did for the radical Left in the 1960s. There is a well-known passage in E. M. Forster's essay, "What I Believe," where he says that if he had to "choose between betraying my country and betraying my friend," he hoped "I should have the guts to betray my country." This was written in 1939, and Forster had witnessed the attempt by both the Nazi and Soviet dictatorships to impose a total commitment and obligation to the state, itself embodying an ideology, which was to override all other commitments and relationships. The world was full of wretched stories of children informing against parents, wives against husbands and possibly also vice versa, friends against friends, all glorying in it. Against this, Forster was in revulsion. He said he believed in personal relations, which in the age of faith, of the clash of creed against creed in which he was sorry to find himself, were regarded as "bourgeois luxuries" to be got rid of so as to make room for dedication to "some movement or cause."

But the passage has most often been taken out of historical context. Country has been read literally as meaning any organized society and its legal order, which perhaps is what Forster meant; and friend has been read to refer not only to the personal loyalties Forster had in mind but also, very much against his sense, to ideologies and causes—precisely what he hated. And so in Forster's dictum, as received if not altogether as intended, we can find a connection between some at least of Mr. Nixon's men and part at least of the radical Left. Ideological imperatives and personal loyalty prevailed over the norms and commands of the legal order. They kept faith with their friends, and had the guts to betray their country.

It is not remarkable that self-righteousness and ideological fixation should be wedded to authoritarian attitudes, and that the temptation to abuse power should arise. What makes the point of contact a significant starting point for inquiry, what is interesting even about the vulgar—because wholly indiscriminate—attempt to turn Watergate into a reproach to liberal opinion, is that Watergate was evidence of a weakened capacity of our legal order to serve as a self-executing safeguard against this sort of abuse of power. The checks and balances of the government, the contrivance, in the words of the 51st *Federalist*, of "the interior structure of the government," so that "its several constituent parts may, by their mutual relations, be the means of keeping each other in their proper places"—this contrivance works reasonably well. The inner structure was meant to insure accountability, and does. But it is accountability by crisis, accountability by trauma, accountability tending to shade into retribution. One would have expected the legal order to have operated to prevent what occurred. It is a first line of defense that has generally held, not always against plain theft, but effectively enough against self-righteous abuse of executive power in the service of ideological or moral ends. It has held in the past, making it unnecessary to reach the battlements and entrenchments of the constitutional checks and balances. It did not hold this time.

I do not pretend to explain Watergate or the Nixon presidency. And I do not propose to understand, for fear that there may be some truth in the saying, *tout comprendre, c'est tout pardonner*. I do not suggest that Watergate was inevitable, but I do suggest that much of what happened to the legal and social order before Watergate was prologue. The scandals of corruption in our history had their climates, their prologues in war-profiteering and in general relaxation of standards. The Vietnam war produced no major scandal of corruption. But it and much that preceded it produced a moral firestorm, which was the prologue to Watergate.

This prologue can be read in the confusions encountered in distinguishing between toleration of conscientious objection and civil disobedience and the proper limits to toleration, under our legal order. Traditionally recognizing a certain autonomy of conscience, our law has allowed some conscientious objections, particularly to war, although not to war alone. And even beyond this autonomy, the legal order may be said to countenance conscientious disobedience, a suspension of legal obligation. Much depends on the law that is in question, the demands it makes of the individual, its foundation in shared values, the kind of disobedience, and the source. The unlawfulness of disobedience to law on sincerely held grounds of conscience is frequently not taken as conclusive proof of the illegitimacy of disobedience. We often consider, rather, that disobedience raises a question about the law at which it is directed, about its effectiveness—that is obvious—but also about its rightness, or at least its utility. The Supreme Court, in *United States* v. *Seeger*,[1] quoted with approval a remark by Chief Justice Hughes that "in the forum of conscience, duty to a moral power higher than the state has always been maintained,"[2] and a passage by Chief Justice Stone, which expressed a similar thought:

> Morals and sound policy require that the state should not violate the conscience of the individual. All our history gives confirmation to the view that liberty of conscience has a moral and social value which makes it worthy of preservation at the hands of the state. So deep is its significance and vital, indeed, is it to the integrity of man's moral and spiritual nature that nothing short of self-preservation of the state should warrant its violation; and it may well be questioned whether the state which preserves its life by a settled policy of violation of the conscience of the individual will not in fact ultimately lose it by the process.[3]

Thus the current Selective Service Act exempts from "combatant training and service" any person "who, by reason of religious training and belief, is conscientiously opposed to partic-

1. United States v. Seeger, 380 U.S. 163, 169–70 (1965).
2. United States v. Macintosh, 283 U.S. 605 (1931).
3. Harlan Stone, "The Conscientious Objector," 21 *Columbia University Quarterly* 253, 269 (1919), cited in United States v. Seeger, 380 U.S. at 170.

ipation in war in any form."[4] The Supreme Court, in *Seeger*, held that a person who professed no allegiance to any organized religion could be entitled to exemption if his belief held a place in his life parallel to that filled by God among others qualifying for the exemption. Objection to one war in particular—selective objection—was disallowed as a ground. A prudential argument in favor of exempting religious objection to all war is in line with a balancing approach; pacifism, unlike other practices such as plural marriage or sacrifice of first-born children—in behalf of which freedom of religious conscience has also been invoked— is not a moral affront and inflicts no personal harm, and past experience affords reasonable assurance, further, that exemption for sincere pacifists is inherently limited and, hence, unlikely to inflict significant social harm. The argument for exempting pacifists, which has been traditionally accepted by Congress, remains a matter of grace, however, not of constitutional guaranty. In a day when the moral element in countless political issues is singled out as decisive so often by so many, it is not surprising that a certain caution on this matter has commended itself to the Court, else the binding force of law might come to depend on the inclinations of millions of individual consciences, with marked effect on the viability of organized government. "I had assumed," said Justice Douglas in a dissent, "that the welfare of the single human soul was the ultimate test of the vitality of the First Amendment."[5] In the opinion of eight of his colleagues that was saying a bit much. Regrettably, perhaps; but a bit much. While a distinction between pacifist and selective objection may not commend itself to many a sensitive conscience, it is a logical one for the legal order to make. If the law itself provided that those who disagree with it for one or another ordinary reason may disregard it, the law would not be law in any significant sense, but merely another expression of opinion. As a formal proposition that seems to me a necessary conclusion, and it has its considerable practical consequences. Law is the majority will or otherwise an authori-

4. Universal Military Training and Service Act, 62 Stat. 604, 50 U.S.C.A. App. 456.
5. Gillette v. United States, 401 U.S. 437, 469 (1971).

tative norm, coercively expressed; it can permit only restricted room for disagreement with, and exemption from, itself.

As Hannah Arendt has written and I have just implied, "conscientious objection can become politically significant when a number of consciences happen to coincide and the conscientious objectors decide to enter the marketplace and make their voices heard in public."[6] There is then necessarily implicit a challenge to the law objected to, or at least the legal order perceives such a widespread manifestation of conscientious objection as a challenge to the law, and the objectors are assimilated to the ranks of civil disobedients. As to civil disobedience, there is much conduct that bears its appearance and that in other, more unitary systems, which do not diffuse power and lawmaking authority, would indeed be civil disobedience. With us a great deal of such conduct is not; in our federation there are laws within laws and laws above laws. One system of laws which is valid and fully authoritative within itself may be called into question by appeal to another, generally superior, system; and in some measure the reverse is true. It is possible, therefore, for men to behave in a manner which is lawful or may turn out to be, but which is not recognized as such by the legitimate authority in one or another place, and therefore constitutes defiance of that authority and causes disorder. Such behavior, which in a unitary system would be civil disobedience, is often invited by the many-tiered process of law formation characteristic of our own system.

In the spring of 1961, for example, groups of young people rode some integrated buses from a border state into the deep South. The substantive federal law, statutory and constitutional, forbade the segregation of passengers in interstate travel by local statute, ordinance, or administrative action, or by the private choice of the carrier;[7] and these freedom rides were unquestionably interstate travel. The law was clear, but in much of the

6. Hannah Arendt, "Civil Disobedience," in *Is Law Dead?*, ed. Eugene Rostow (New York: Simon and Schuster, 1971), pp. 219–20.

7. See, e.g., Hall v. DeCuir, 95 U.S. 485 (1877); Morgan v. Virginia, 328 U.S. 373 (1946); Mitchell v. United States, 313 U.S. 80 (1941); Henderson v. United States, 339 U.S. 816 (1950); Boynton v. Virginia, 364 U.S. 454 (1960).

South it was not accepted, or established, or observed. To achieve more secure establishment and more effective enforcement of the superior federal law when it is flouted by inferior sovereignty of the state, one might be expected to rely on the orderly process of litigation or the political process, which can produce remedial legislation; but not on a disorderly process of mass self-help, as the freedom riders did. In fact, our system accepts both orderly and disorderly processes; and almost, it could be said, offers an incentive to disorderly process, in the sense that jurisdictional and procedural rules of litigation tend to demand a concrete, not suppositional, clash between federal law and local practice.[8] Defiant self-help is a legitimate method, and constitutes a right whose exercise has a claim to protection at the hands of federal authority—a claim President John F. Kennedy honored in defense of the safety of the freedom riders.

The system similarly invites and countenances a disorderly, self-help method of formation of new substantive law, as well. In February 1960, Negro students who walked in and sat peaceably at segregated lunch counters in Greensboro, North Carolina, were refused service and arrested by local police for violation of the property rights of the private lunch-counter operators. It disturbed the peace of the community. The students argued that the local law, while valid and enforceable locally for the time being, should not be and would not long prove to be when tested by those willing to bet on its ultimate invalidity. This was an exercise in law formation through exploitation of the natural tension between two coexisting systems of law, state and federal. In a unitary state this might have been seen as an act of conscience, an appeal to higher law, but certainly an act of disobedience, perhaps a revolutionary act, at war with the legal order. In our own federal system, the appeal to higher law is not a call for revolutionary change, or simply some cry from the heart; it is a practical appeal in almost a technical, legal sense, to existing higher law-making institutions. The sit-ins did not win in the federal courts,

8. See United Public Workers v. Mitchell, 330 U.S. 75 (1947); Rescue Army v. Municipal Court, 331 U.S. 549 (1947); Poe v. Ullman, 367 U.S. 497 (1961). Compare Griswold v. Connecticut, 381 U.S. 479 (1965).

as it happened; the Supreme Court never did declare a constitutional right to equal service in private places of public accommodation. Instead, the sit-ins gained enactment of Title II of the Civil Rights Act of 1964, a legislative creation, under the commerce clause of the Constitution, recognizing a right to service in places of public accommodation. Had the Supreme Court held segregation in private places of public accommodation unconstitutional, all pending state court convictions of the students would have fallen. And yet the Supreme Court did find a way to achieve a similar result, albeit with a certain strain. It held that the Civil Rights Act implicitly forgave, abated, as if by an amnesty, convictions still pending on appeal in nonviolent sit-in cases now covered by the Act.[9] And in many communities, where the sit-ins had succeeded in forming new local law by voluntary concession, prosecutions were often dropped.

Another remarkable example of self-help had occurred during the Second World War in an appeal not from local law but from the federal legislature to the federal judiciary. After the Selective Service Act of 1940 was passed, leaders of the German-American Bund "commanded" their members to refuse military service: to register as required, but to refuse induction. The Bund leaders, including the Bund's counsel, argued that a certain provision of the draft law made the entire law unconstitutional; resistance to it would result in a test of its validity. The leaders were convicted of conspiring to counsel their membership to evade service in the armed forces, but the Supreme Court reversed the conviction. The defendants' view that the draft law was unconstitutional was "foolish," the Court said, but the evidence showed that it was nonetheless sincerely held. The defendants did not counsel their members not to register, thus seeking to evade the draft "stealthily and by guile." To provoke a court test of their own constitutional theory, however mistaken, was not evasion, and not punishable.[10]

9. Hamm v. City of Rock Hill, 379 U.S. 306 (1964).

10. Keegan v. United States, 325 U.S. 478 (1945); see Okamoto v. United States, 152 F. 2d 905 (10th Cir. 1946); cf. Gara v. United States, 178 F. 2d 38 (6th Cir. 1949).

A general definition of civil disobedience, applicable to our legal order, would be the following: Civil disobedience is the act of disobeying formally binding general law on grounds of moral or political principle without challenging the validity of the law; or the incidental disobedience of general law, which is itself neither challenged as invalid nor disapproved of, in the course of agitating for change in public policies, actions, or social conditions which are regarded as bad on grounds of moral or political principle—all in circumstances where the legal order makes no allowance for the disobedience. This last qualification has to be added because the First Amendment is construed as making some allowance for the sort of incidental disobedience referred to in the second half of the definition. In purpose, if not in effect, civil disobedience differs greatly from conscientious objection.

The effect of the coincidence of multiple consciences objecting to a law and the effect of civil disobedience may be the same. But conscientious objection is a withdrawal. Civil disobedience is ineluctably an attempt to coerce the legal order, an exercise of power in the sense in which Burke defined it: "Liberty, when men act in bodies, is *power*." And it is not easy to make room for it, although our legal order does so. Neither the Hobbesian nor the contractarian view of the nature and foundation of society, however, can tolerate civil disobedience, the contractarian view because it legitimates government as a compact among citizens, embodying the agreement of each to abide the judgment of all in behalf of substantially predetermined ends that are limited by timeless principles, the rights of man. Government is allowed some margin of error, but the premise is that it will normally act only in plausible pursuit of these predetermined ends. If it should not, says Locke, the remedy is revolution. Short of the right of revolution, there is an absolute duty to obey. Rousseau held that the people, expressing themselves through universal suffrage, give voice to the general will, although he allowed that they might also not. The general will is the highest good, and when the people by majority vote give it voice, the individual owes obedience even unto death. If a minority at times has hold of the true general will, absolute obedience is equally owed to it. This, said Rousseau, only forces the individual to be free.

The latest contribution to contractarian theory, by Rawls in *A Theory of Justice*,[11] also posits a general will—called justice as fairness—and commits government to its effectuation. Like Rousseau, it insists on popular sovereignty, modified only by some power in the judges to keep government within the limits dictated by the general will. And it posits a duty to obey. But it makes allowance, one may think inconsistently, for civil disobedience, with the proviso that it be public and willing to accept punishment. Civil disobedience is allowed because, it turns out, the general will is not always readily ascertainable, the majority and the judges may be wrong—or less right than a protesting minority—and civil disobedience can help the entire society decide what is right. In that event, it would seem, there is less to the definition of justice as fairness than meets the eye.

In the actual American legal order, ends are less permanently predetermined than by contractarian theory, faith in majoritarianism is less enthusiastic than Rousseau's, readiness to have recourse to revolution is not as great as Locke's, and there is little willingness to accept the righteous dictates of a minority possessed of the true general will. What is above all important is consent—not a presumed theoretical consent but a continuous actual one, born of continual responsiveness. There is popular sovereignty, and there are votes in which majorities or pluralities prevail. But that is not nearly all, for majorities are in large part fictions. They exist only on election day and they can be registered on very few issues. To be responsive and to enjoy consent, government must register numerous expressions of need and interest by numerous groups, and it must register relative intensities of need and interest. Neither the vote nor speech—the latter, after all, an elite exercise—sufficiently differentiates needs and interests, or expresses intensity. Civil disobedience can often effectively do so. Hence it is that civil disobedience has accompanied so many of the most

11. John Rawls, *A Theory of Justice* (Cambridge: Harvard University Press, Belknap Press, 1971).

fruitful reform movements in American history. Hence it is that its legitimacy must be recognized.

Stephen A. Douglas had argued in his debates with Abraham Lincoln in 1858 that "whoever resists the final decision of the highest judicial tribunal aims a deadly blow at our whole republican system of government." "I yield obedience," Douglas said, "to the decisions of that Court—to the final determination of the highest judicial tribunal known to our Constitution." But the Court does not issue Holy Writ, it can be wrong, Lincoln responded, and men may properly differ with the Court. "If I were in Congress," said Lincoln, "and a vote should come up on a question whether slavery should be prohibited in a new territory in spite of that Dred Scott decision, I would vote that it should." That was ridiculous, cried Douglas, "I never heard before of an appeal being taken from the Supreme Court." And there's the heart of the matter. Appeals *can* be taken from the Supreme Court, as Lincoln knew. Douglas, he said, "would have the citizen conform his vote to that decision; the member of Congress, his; the President, his use of the veto power. He would make it a rule of political action for the people and all the departments of government. I would not. By resisting it as a political rule, I disturb no right of property, create no disorder, excite no mobs."[12] If no one acts contrary to its decision, the Court may never have a chance to reverse.

Lincoln's position did not lack precedent, and one precedent had been supplied by Taney himself, the author of the Dred Scott decision,[13] when he was Attorney General of the United States. A judgment of the Supreme Court, he said, is conclusive of the case in which it is rendered, but "it does not follow that the reasoning or principles which [the Court] announced in coming to its conclusion are equally binding and obligatory" on the legislative and executive branches. Those branches may believe the Court's principles and reasoning to be erroneous, and in that

12. Paul Angle, ed., *Created Equal: The Complete Lincoln-Douglas Debates of 1858* (Chicago: University of Chicago Press, 1958), passim.
13. Scott v. Sandford, 60 U.S. (19 Howard) 393 (1857).

event need not conform to them.[14] Liberals, conservatives, popu-
lists, slave owners, capitalists, socialists—everybody at one time
or another has acted on the Taney-Lincoln view of what the
meaning of a constitutional decision really is. The absence of any
identification of this view in our history with any group, interest,
ideology, or political outlook gives great assurance of its
correctness.

The legal order takes account of and may respond to individual
moral acts of selective objection for which it cannot make formal
allowance. Such acts are not illegitimate to the operation of the
legal order, the mechanism of giving or withholding the consent
which the order subsumes. For although we govern by majority
rule, it is with the consent of the minority. If the minority believes
with sufficient intensity that the majority is wrong, the majority
may find it too costly to enforce its will. This is especially true
if what the majority seeks to do requires not simply the minority's
silent acquiescence but its active participation. A minority's resistance may cause a majority—unpersuaded and intact in numbers—to reexamine its position and to recede from it.

These are exercises in negative law formation. I had nearly
said nullification, to which might be added the achievement, however qualified, of the antiwar movement in toppling a sitting
president, in the midst of war, in 1968, before a single national
vote had been cast. A democratic state which fights with a conscripted popular army, as most states like ours have done since
the French Revolution, will do so effectively with difficulty when
a large and intense body of opinion, particularly among those of
fighting age, resolutely opposes the war on moral and political
grounds. A conscripted army requires more than majority political
decision to fight a war, which is one reason why the idea of a
volunteer army must be regarded with misgiving. To use mer-
cenary armies is to weaken this built-in, systemic restraint. But in
numerous other ways as well, the waging of war needs continuous

14. See Carl Swisher, "Mr. Chief Justice Taney," in *Mr. Justice,* ed.
Allison Dunham and Philip B. Kurland (Chicago: University of Chicago
Press, 1964), pp. 209–12.

political support; it is subject to a continuous round of informal referenda. A democracy cannot well wage a war—as witness the earlier examples of the War of 1812 and the Mexican War—and should not wage a war which a substantial and intense body of opinion resolutely opposes on both political and moral grounds. Even autocracies cannot effectively wage wars in such circumstances. Congress may declare war by the narrowest of majorities, and no individual is legally—though he may well be morally—entitled to nullify application to himself of a declaration of war because he disagrees with it, any more than he can do so when it comes to other disagreeable laws passed by narrow divisions. The majority is not limited to expressions of opinion. It is entitled to make law. To register opposition that may overturn the majority's law, therefore, is to invite punishment. Still, those who govern are required to exercise forbearance and continence, without which law cannot be effective, or on some occasions just. "It is not," said Burke to the government of King George III in his second speech on conciliation with America, "what a lawyer tells me I *may* do; but what humanity, reason, and justice tell me I ought to do." The fact is that no measures of pervasive application can or should rest on narrow majorities. These are the limits of effective legal action, and they bear with particular force on the making of war.

Even after the majority has exacted penalties for opposition, and perhaps the more so when it has, the legal order may respond to the ground of objection by reconsideration of its own decision. To the extent that this occurs we witness the process of law formation. Costly for the individual and fraught with risks for the society, it is nevertheless a legitimate part of a process which is concerned to register intensity rather than numbers. A well-advised and reflective individual considering resistance will acknowledge and weigh other obligations: to the country whose institutions and ways he may in general value, despite its present error; to the country in a more abstract sense, as parent, as Socrates says in the *Crito*; to fellow countrymen who do go and fight; above all, and as the sum of it all, to the judgment embodied in a majority decision, which deserves at least provisional, presumptive respect balanced against a too readily self-righteous conscience. Too little decent respect for the opinion of his fellow-countrymen is the moral danger that the prospective conscientious objector confronts. For conscientious objection—and I do not derogate the moral courage it demands even as I emphasize the moral danger it presents—is a decision in favor of self, in favor of the idea of self. The individual must try to step outside himself long enough to conceive of his decision multiplied many times over in situations other than his own. If some men may follow conscience, all men may.

Consider this example, a story from Atlanta reported in the *New York Times* of January 4, 1972. A middle-class white father, characterized as distraught because busing was employed to attain better racial balance in the schools, had rented an apartment elsewhere, leaving it vacant but using the address as a subterfuge to keep his child out of the inner city schools to which she was assigned. He was quoted as saying that his child "has a right not to be carted 30 miles a day for an education. If I have to break a law to see that she isn't, then I will—and that's what I'm doing, I suppose." If the legal order is as I describe it, relatively open and reachable, taking account of a participatory process of law formation, this determined parent must be allowed into the circle. What possible distinction, other than a personal, predilectional one, exists between his position and that of the selective conscientious objector?

Not every law, of course, does have a moral dimension, not every law can plausibly be said to offend anyone's conscience, nor need the moral realm be left wholly to subjective definition. We can as a society and a culture discover some boundaries. Society is to judge, and the legal order does judge, formally or informally, whether the moral claim is plausible. And the response of the legal order to genuine acts of conscience, and even to widespread ones, varies; there is a calculus into which the moral intensity of the objector, the moral weight of his objection, and the moral foundation of the law all enter. We ought to be capable of judging, and we certainly undertake to judge, as we have to, the sincerity of an act of conscience—whether its moral claim is within the realm of plausible moral claims. The further qualitative judgment is more difficult, and equally time- and culture-bound, but if it cannot be made with a reasonable measure of objectivity and validity, not in the eye of eternity but for our time and our place, we are not a viable society. We do make such judgments continually, on and off the Supreme Court, with due and sober realization, one hopes—to paraphrase a saying of Justice Holmes —with due realization that time may upset them, but with fair confidence for the time being. We could not go on otherwise. As we are required to judge claims of conscience by the quality and magnitude of the moral issue on which they rest, so we are equally required, in an extension of the function performed by the Supreme Court in many First Amendment cases, to judge whether failure to observe law is ordinarily antisocial behavior, or rather, is grounded in a plausible claim that the law is bad on principle because it is arguably inconsistent with the values of the legal order itself. If the latter is the case, disobedience is not simply a deplorable malfunction but may be a legitimate part of the process of the formation of law if it is legitimate in manner as well.

The Court, an independent body of men, not responsible or responsive after the fashion of democratic institutions but answerable only, as Chief Justice Warren pointed out in his farewell remarks, each to his conscience, is not only an effective instrument for ensuring fairness and justice in the government's dealings with the individual, but a splendid instrument for forcing the society's attention to issues of principle, particularly issues of moral principle that often are submerged in the welter of affairs. When such a body of men goes farther, not merely to expose issues of principle but to impose its own resolutions of them, the consequences may again be beneficial. Of that, posterity is the judge. But contemporaneous doubts are rooted in the democratic faith, which holds that the society at large ought to participate in the venture of governing itself, and that the general good is achieved by pragmatic trial and error—having regard to principle, but not dogmatically bound to it in action—which is the genius of democratic institutions. Now and again, the Court succeeds in doing great

and enduring work in the teeth of such doubts. This was largely
the case with the nationalizing work of John Marshall's Court.
But it has not often been the case in other periods when the
Supreme Court has undertaken to form and put into effect major
policies. Hence the doubts not only persist but are strengthened
by the past history of the Court. A Court sensitive to these doubts
tends to attack problems at retail, in the smallest possible compass, illuminating ultimate principles in the glare of its headlights,
as it were, but seldom speeding ahead to seize such principles
and to deploy them for the definitive, authoritative resolution of
large social and political issues. We will return finally to the truth
that laws are not always effective simply because they are there.
To think so is to forget what a great legal scholar, Roscoe Pound,
called "the limits of effective legal action,"[15] to forget that only
in a certain kind of social and political situation is law self-
executing through its own institutions, and that there are times
when extralegal resources must be brought to the aid of the law if
it is to attain its end. Enactment and enforcement of law are
sometimes only episodes, even if the single most important and
influential ones, in a long and varied process by which society,
working through a number of institutions, manages to realize a
given purpose.

The limits of law, then, are the limits of enforcement, and the
limits of enforcement are the conditions of a free society; perhaps, indeed, the limit of government altogether. If substantial
portions of the statute book had to be enforced by direct action—
whether through civil or criminal litigation—against large numbers of people, we would have a very different and infinitely more
disagreeable society than we do. To be sure, there is always a
residuum of the antisocial, whose numbers the enforcement
process, most often the criminal process, strives to reduce, although never with absolute success. And there may be laws,
such as narcotics statutes, which some people may be simply in-

15. Roscoe Pound, "Address Before the Pennsylvania Bar Association," 22 *Pennsylvania Bar Association Report* 221 (1916).

capable of obeying. Still, laws about killing and stealing, about the payment of taxes, about contracts, about torts, about labor relations, and even traffic laws, are effectively, if never absolutely, in force. And yet we have a free society, not a police state. We invest limited resources in the effort to enforce law, and we sacrifice few other values in the process. The secret of this enterprise is that most people, most of the time, need only to be made aware of the law in order to obey it. Much litigation is the consequence of differences of opinion about what the law is or ought to be, not of failure to obey what is clearly the law.

In a simple system when, as Pound pointed out, "men demand little of law and enforcement of law is but enforcement of the ethical minimum necessary for the orderly conduct of society, enforcement of law involves few difficulties. All but the inevitable anti-social residuum can understand the simple program and obvious purposes of such a legal system," he said.

> On the other hand, when men demand much of law, when they seek to devolve upon it the whole burden of social control, when they seek to make it do the work of the home and of the church, enforcement of law comes to involve many difficulties. . . . The purposes of the legal order are [then] not all upon the surface and it may be that many whose nature is by no means anti-social are out of accord with some or even with many of these purposes. . . . [It is then that] we begin to hear complaint that laws are not enforced and the forgotten problem of the limitations upon effective legal action once more becomes acute.[16]

Although laws, very nearly all laws, are readily accorded general acquiescence, and are easily effective, there are times when law does not gain general consent merely by virtue of having been authoritatively pronounced, and lacking such consent it cannot be effective—such failure is demonstrated by anti-

16. Ibid., pp. 222, 232.

gambling statutes, which coexist with widespread gambling, and by laws regulating common sexual practices, which lie largely in disuse.

When people in the millions or even hundreds of thousands are opposed—intensely, consistently, and on principle—to a law bearing directly on their conduct of ordinary affairs; effective enforcement is possible, if at all, only through military occupation. Effective enforcement in the face of determined and widespread opposition is possible only if the private conduct that is to be regulated is subject to more or less continuous official scrutiny, and to more or less continuous coercion. It makes no difference that the opposition is nationally in a minority. As Walter Lippmann remarked in 1926, writing about Prohibition, "when the object is to regulate personal habit and social custom, the majority which matters is the majority of the community concerned." People in the sort of numbers we are talking about will control some state governments and many other local authorities, and these in turn may decline to cooperate in the enforcement of locally unpopular federal law. But the chief source of the difficulty is not that the federal government lacks the basic police power and is helpless without the cooperation of the states. The heart of the matter is that no normal police and prosecuting activity can be effective in such circumstances, nothing short of the pervasive presence of armed men will do. When elementary public order breaks down, such a presence has proved necessary in the past as a temporary measure; may be necessary on future occasions; and is well within the authority and capability of the federal government. But as a regular and more or less permanent device, it is something from which we recoil, deeming it destructive of the values of a free society and in the end, quite possibly, counterproductive even in terms of its immediate aim. The true alternatives, therefore, are to reduce the opposition by a process of inducement and persuasion, or to abandon the law. Abandonment of the law is not inconsistent with occasional enforcement in pitched circumstances. And abandonment does not have to be formal, at least not immediately; the law may stay on the books for a while, it may even be observed in some parts of the country, but if it is substantially abandoned in practice, that in the end is what really matters. Noncompliance is contagious, and the statute-book will conform to the practice.

Dramatic proof of the proposition may be drawn from two notorious experiences in American history, one the Fugitive Slave Law, the other the Eighteenth Amendment. The Fugitive Slave Act of 1850 was part of that year's broad compromise on the slavery problem, engineered by Henry Clay and seconded by Daniel Webster, an act with firm support in the Constitution, but repugnant to much of the North. Emerson, no wild abolitionist, called it "this filthy enactment." and wrote in his journal: "I will not obey it, by God!" Many Northern states passed "personal liberty laws," as they were called, which were inconsistent with the act, thinly veiled attempts to nullify it. Efforts at enforcement were often resisted by mobs, were in any event not significant, and soon virtually ceased. A hardening and broadening of Northern antislavery sentiment was the result. Nearly three-quarters of a century later, Prohibition was imposed on the country by constitutional amendment, proposed by the necessary two-thirds vote of the Congress, and ratified by the legislatures of ten more states than necessary, forty-six in all. Because some thought the Eighteenth Amendment might, paradoxically, be unconstitutional, the question was carried to the Supreme Court, but the Court held otherwise.[17] In some states Prohibition was effective; in other areas enforcement soon became a shambles. The Volstead Act was, of course, openly disdained. Respectable and substantial people advised violation of it, and public officials condoned violation. Leaders of opinion began to talk of nullification. No enforcement was possible; the law was no law.

What do these ominous lessons from history teach us? It is first to be remarked that the Fugitive Slave Act *was* an immoral law, and that the Eighteenth Amendment attempted to regulate conduct that is morally neutral, and as to which one's neighbor or a majority of one's countrymen ought, of right, have no power to impose their views. Such judgments are not to be escaped; they

17. National Prohibition Cases, 253 U.S. 350 (1920).

are always decisive. That is the blunt truth, and we may as well be aware of it. If, on the other hand, a law is a just law, embodying minimal moral requirements that a national majority may properly attempt to impose, then the earlier experiences teach that persuasion and inducement, tasks of political and social leadership and education, must intervene to generate consent and compel obedience. Pronouncement of the law is the first step, and in itself an important persuasive and educational action.

In 1954–55, in *Brown* v. *Board of Education*,[18] the Supreme Court held that at least legally enforced segregation is unconstitutional and must be stopped and disestablished. It is often and easily assumed, however, and the Court at times has shared this assumption, that a rule of constitutional law laid down by the Supreme Court becomes immediately the law of the land, that if it is not, it should be; else the result is a failure of the system, a failure of enforcement, a failure of nerve. In the Little Rock case of 1957,[19] the first school desegregation case after *Brown* to reach it, the Court said a constitutional rule once laid down by the Supreme Court creates a duty among all persons affected, and especially government officials who are oathbound to effectuate the Court's will to implement that law. The Court did not say that citizens in general are under an obligation to obey the Court's law, but that was the clear implication. When the Court's law affects limited interests and its prestige is sufficient to gain general acquiescence in its will, that *is* how things work; but not when the Court's judgments touch points of serious stress in the society. For the basis of all law—judicial, legislative, or administrative—is consensual. We are willing, and ought to be willing, to pay only a limited price in coercing minorities. Whenever a minority is sufficiently large or determined or, as in the case of *Brown*, strategically placed, we do not quite have law. We must then generate a greater measure of consent, or reconsider our stance on the minority's position. We must, in such circumstances, resort to methods other than coercive law; methods of persuasion

18. Brown v. Board of Education, 347 U.S. 483 (1954).
19. Cooper v. Aaron, 358 U.S. 1 (1958).

and inducement, appeal to reason and shared values, appeal to interest, and not only material but political interest. We act on the realization that the law needs to be established before it can be effectively enforced, that it is, in a quite real sense, still provisional.

The crucial point is that we engage in a contest of wills. If a majority relaxes in a failure of patience or in discontinuity of purpose as it did after Reconstruction, or if it thinks it can devolve its responsibility on some enforcement officials in Washington and forget about it, as it largely did during Reconstruction, the law is from that moment moribund. If it could have been understood that the Court's decision in *Brown* and the passage of the civil rights statutes launched a great reforming enterprise, to be carried on by the society as a whole and not merely by the enforcing arm of the federal government, success could at least be possible. Without that common effort such an enterprise may fail. The general practice is to leave the enforcement of judge-made constitutional law to private initiative, and to enforce it case by case, so that no penalties attach to failure to abide by it before completion of a successful enforcement litigation. This means quite literally that no one is under any legal obligation to carry out a rule of constitutional law announced by the Supreme Court until someone else has conducted a successful litigation and obtained a decree directing him to do so. Any rule of constitutional law not put into effect voluntarily by officials and other persons who acquiesce in it, or not taken up by legislation and made more effective by administrative or noncoercive means—any such rule is not in our system an effective rule of law. If there is widespread nonobservance, the resources neither of private litigating initiative nor of the judicial process as such are equal to making it effective. The Court thus interacts with other institutions, with whom it is engaged in an endlessly renewed educational conversation. It is a conversation that takes place when statutes are construed, when jurisdiction is defined and perhaps declined, when the lower federal courts are addressed by the Supreme Court as their "administrative head," and also when large "constitutional issues" are decided. And it is a conversation, not a monologue.

Moral Duty and the Limits
of Civil Disobedience

Limits to conscientious objection and to civil disobedience must be stated not as positive law imposed by the enforcement machinery of the legal order, but as a moral obligation, a duty to obey. Use of the enforcement machinery of the legal order denotes the point at which it has broken down; the test of a legal order is its self-executing capacity, its moral authority. In an extraordinarily sustained experience of civil disobedience and conscientious objection on the part of at least three distinct, sizable groups in the society over a period of some fifteen years—which perhaps no other society could have endured without a change of re-gime—in this sustained experience, the limits were often trans-gressed. The experience started with white Southerners in the mid-fifties; it was followed and overlapped by the civil rights movement; and it ended with and was overlapped by the white-middle-class movement against the Vietnam war. The limits were transgressed, and in some measure, I am willing to suggest, Watergate was a replica of the transgressions.

A first and most easily stated limit was very clear to Lincoln when he said of the *Dred Scott* decision that "We do not propose that when Dred Scott has been decided to be a slave by the court, we as a mob will decide him to be free . . . but we nevertheless do oppose that decision as a political rule which shall be binding." The line was thus drawn between the general law, the law of the land, enunciated in a judicial decision, or *mutatis mutandis* in legislation, and the judicial judgment addressed to the parties in an actual case. There is no moral duty always and invariably to obey the former. There is a moral duty to obey the latter. The limit of moral duty to obey judicial judgment in an actual case was transgressed repeatedly in the South during the fifties and sixties, by private and official persons, and by mobs who disobeyed or violated judicial decrees. It was transgressed as well by disruptive courtroom behavior on the part of the radical Left in the late sixties which amounted to the same thing, denoting as it did a rejection of the process and necessarily, therefore, of its results. Both kinds of transgression were perhaps more spectacular than numerous, but they told.

Another sort of limit on civil disobedience has to do with means. Violence must be a monopoly of the state. In private hands, whatever its possible misuses by the state, it is always an unjust weapon. It is inadmissible, but has been widely used and excused. The historian Gabriel Kolko said of the man who planted a bomb in 1970 at the University of Wisconsin's Mathematics Research Center, which killed one person and wounded four: "To condemn Karl Armstrong is to condemn a whole anguished generation. His intentions were more significant than the unanticipated consequences of his actions." Yet the extended consequences could be foreseen in that our freedom is founded ultimately on respect for moral values and for law. Enough violent disorder, and men with helmets and guns will patrol the streets. Enough violent disorder, and the leaders of groups inciting to violence will be rounded up—on proper warrants; and put behind bars— after proper trials, having first been held on proper high bail. And where courts are violently disrupted and judges assaulted, it may not be possible to consider that they are functioning in the "unobstructed exercise of their jurisdiction," and then full-fledged martial law, with trials before military commissions, may follow. Under our Constitution, the United States would have great difficulty turning itself into a repressive society. But no American chief executive is likely to regard himself as having been elected to preside over the dissolution of the government. Lincoln didn't. Some nonviolent interference with the justified and lawful activities and expectations of innocent third parties is an inevitable concomitant of civil disobedience and, if contained and civil, is to be borne, subject to other limits to which I shall come. But when the interference is massive, when it is not civil, when it borders on violence or threatens it, when it is coercive not in its ultimate intent—as all civil disobedience necessarily is—but in its immediate impact, when its imposition is not of inconvenience but of terror, then it is unacceptable. And yet we have seen quantities of it.

The possibility of violence not caused or provoked by civil disobedients, but predictably drawn by them from others—a violent veto—under the First Amendment, is, however, no argument against activity otherwise legitimate or tolerable. The responsibility of government is to counter the violence at its source, not to act against its victims, excepting only to prevent a violent disaster.

Additional limits to civil disobedience, at least equally important, are much more difficult to state. One, also having to do with means, is suggested by the action of Daniel Ellsberg in using his position of trust to spirit out the Pentagon Papers, or the action of the unknown person who handed to columnist Jack Anderson a transcript of a secret meeting on the India-Pakistan war, presided over by Henry Kissinger at the White House. There is in such cases the question whether a legal obligation was breached. This was and remains a question in some doubt in both the examples, which the aborted Ellsberg litigation did not settle. I assume, strictly for purposes of argument, that a legal obligation was breached, although in truth I believe it to be quite doubtful that there is on the books a statute that effectively renders illegal what Ellsberg, for example, did. At any rate, these were acts of conscience taken against at least a privately formulated obligation. They were taken in conditions where conscience could have been satisfied in part by resignation. I have in mind a situation in which the legal order does not demand participation in the society's morally objectionable enterprise, as in the case of a government employee who gives the transcript of the secret meeting on the India-Pakistan war to Jack Anderson, or who hands over the personnel file of an ambassador to Senator Joseph R. McCarthy, or in the case of a senator's assistant who disgorges his employer's files to Jack Anderson's predecessor in title, the late Drew Pearson. These can all quite plausibly be viewed as acts of conscience. But if I don't like how Henry Kissinger runs a meeting, I can tell him off to his face, and then resign. If I don't like the way the State Department runs, I can resign from the State Department and join Joe McCarthy. And if I don't like my senatorial boss, I can quit.

Ellsberg and the unknown persons who gave Jack Anderson the secret India-Pakistan transcript or the files to Drew Pearson allowed their consciences to push them into more affirmative action. That was not because as moral beings they could do no other. It was rather because they wanted to make others do otherwise than they were doing. Their acts, unaided by other independent consciences, had a different and greater impact than ordinary conscientious objection—I should say a coercive impact—lent them by the trust that had been reposed in the actors personally. These actors were not denying the legal order their own participation in its immoral activity, as they viewed it. They sought rather to coerce the legal order by destroying *pro tanto* the procedures by which it conducts its business.

I do not say that such acts can never be justified. Suppose Ellsberg had discovered evidence of plans to herd people into concentration camps and gas them, or evidence of treason? These, however, are examples of an extreme kind of moral outbreak activating the individual. My point is that impositional, coercive acts of conscience of this sort should require a much higher moral threshold than does passive conscientious objection, and I do not believe it was clear in either the Ellsberg or the Kissinger secret-meeting case that the threshold had been reached. Certainly the Vietnam war raised moral issues. But the secrecy of the Pentagon Papers did not raise the same ones, by any means, even though the mendacity of government is a serious matter. And it was self-deception to think that release of the Papers would solve the moral problem of the war. Anyone contemplating an impositional coercive act of conscience must recognize orders of magnitude among moral questions. An insufficiently differentiated exaltation of wrongs to the same moral level is quite entirely the same as, and no less dangerous than, moral blindness. In the case of the person who gave the secret transcript to Jack Anderson, the issue was not one to which a single answer could be returned by any person of reasonable disinterest and moral endowment. And for an impositional act of conscience, that must be the standard.

Just as there are circumstances when a breach of duty of the impositional sort committed by Ellsberg could be justified, so conditions arise when extralegal action by a president in the interest of national security is called for. Again, the threshold must be very high. But if challenged, such actions may in the proper circumstances be ratified as legal, if only from necessity, as the removal of Japanese-Americans from the West Coast in 1942 unfortunately was. The principle of legitimation is the simple one stated by Justice Jackson: The Constitution is not a suicide pact. The president has the function at times, even the duty, to see that it does not become one. And even when not ratified by the institutions of the legal order—as the seizure of the steel industry by Harry Truman, or Lincoln's suspension of *habeas corpus*, or martial law in Hawaii in World War II, or domestic wiretapping by presidents from Franklin D. Roosevelt through Nixon were not ratified—such actions are not necessarily condemned. My point is that the threshold for taking them has in the past been enormously high. Legal norms have radiated with powerful force. In a paroxysm of paranoia, to state the case as indulgently as possible, the Nixon administration lowered the threshold. Early on, before Ellsberg, Mr. Nixon and his people may well have sorely abused what they regarded, not unjustly, as wiretapping authority legitimated by practice, and they at least contemplated other outrages, but it cannot be entirely a coincidence that Ellsberg's removal of the Pentagon Papers from the RAND Corporation was the occasion for creation of a so-called White House plumbers unit. Threshold for threshold.

Returning to civil disobedience, let me restate the grounds on which its legitimacy can be rested. It is because on most issues we command no definite answers grounded in solid and generally shared values that we value an open, responsive, varied, and continual process of law formation and provide numerous stages of decision-making, most of them provisional, and numerous opportunities for revision and resistance, including civil disobedience. But not only do the outcomes of the law formation process, however provisional, count for something; what is more important, in the middle distance, and if also provisionally then over a much longer term, we do as a legal order hold some values, some principles, by which we judge the process and even some of its outcomes. Unless these are defended against coercive political action, there is no legal order, or at any rate, there is not this one. The legal order does rest, I believe, on an acceptance of it, regardless of errors and malfunctions. And at this, the irreducible point, acceptance must take the form of an individual duty to obey—voluntarily and prior to coercion. The alternatives are stark: chaos, the brutal domination of the strongest and cruelest; or revolution, a Hobbesian war for a time, and then a legal order whose premises may be differently stated, and some of whose premises may in fact be different, but which must finally acknowledge the same necessities as the present one. No doubt, the committed revolutionary cannot be charged with a duty to obey. He yields no allegiance to the legal order, assigns no value to its coherence and survival. He is in rebellion against it and wishes to see it overthrown, regardless of the consequences. Yet, no matter what Locke said, and Jefferson after him, there can be no right to rebel, except retroactively, following a successful rebellion. In the *Crito* and the *Apology*, Socrates suggests that the law that punished him for corrupting the young by teaching atheism is not an unjust law, that he may well have been guilty of corrupting the young. In parts of the *Apology* he seems to argue that as a philosopher he ought to be allowed to question and corrupt, because a philosopher must. Yet in a corrupt society, Thessaly, "where is found the greatest disorder and license," Socrates would not wish to live. The individual who disobeys a just law pits his judgment against the society's final one, delivered in his own case: Who can trust himself, or be trusted, to be "judge in his own case . . . however righteous his motives."

So conscience is disciplined by risk. A pestilence of indiscriminate, self-righteous, individual moral judgments, coercively imposed on the society, or collective immorality, or amorality, would destroy our legal order as readily as would a moral obtuseness. Therefore, the use of civil disobedience, not to redress grievances on the assumption of the continued operation of the system and by plausible appeal to its own principles, but against it, ought not be tolerated. Civil disobedience is one thing, revolutionary activity quite another, and the difference between them is told not only by their manner but also by their objectives.

This distinction is rigorously drawn by Rawls in his *A Theory of Justice*, to which I have referred. The distinction was not drawn in the sixties with anything like Mr. Rawl's rigor. Much of the disobedience then was aimed not at the government of the day but at the system, and it opposed the system not as flawed and perfectible but as evil and abominable. The rhetoric abandoned all pretense of allegiance, it acknowledged no restraint and no bounds. Yet it was often tolerated and even echoed by seemingly responsible opinion in the press, in the universities, and among political leaders. Cries of repression and of fascism, for example, were raised almost as soon as Mr. Nixon took office, and they were irresponsible and unfounded at the time, no matter how plausible they may seem in retrospect. At the time, they were bound to have an effect on administration morale. Men who are loudly charged with repression before they have done anything to substantiate the charge are apt to proceed to substantiate it.

In a larger sense, toleration of disobedience with such aims undermined the moral authority of the liberal tradition in this country, which as Louis Hartz pointed out years ago is at once also the American conservative tradition, or at least the tradition that conserves the liberal American legal and political order. Hartz quoted the distinguished insight of Gunnar Myrdal: "America is . . . conservative. . . . But the principles conserved are liberal and some, indeed, are radical."[20] Liberalism has always been challenged from both flanks and has always been a little anxious, like the Center of the Third French Republic, to make no enemies on the Left. Indeed, it has historically been successful in coopting all but the revolutionary Left, moving far enough toward it to draw its sympathizers and outriders, but generally not so far as to be itself coopted. To move too far would be to lose moral authority, and that rather than numbers is

20. Louis Hartz, *The Liberal Tradition in America* (New York: Harcourt, Brace and Co., 1955), p. 50.

the source of the liberal ascendancy in American politics which safeguards the norms of the American legal order against the lawlessness and ultimate authoritarianism of radical movements. In the forties liberalism embraced too much of the Left, and the result was the triumph for a moment of the radicalism of Joseph R. McCarthy. In this same sense Watergate was to American liberalism as McCarthyism was.

In the process still another necessary limit of civil disobedience was transgressed. Like law itself, civil disobedience is habit-forming, and the habit it forms is destructive of the legal order. Disobedience, even if legitimate in every other way, must not be allowed to become epidemic. Individuals are under a duty to ration themselves, to assess occasions in terms of their relative as well as absolute importance. Anybody who wishes responsive government, a society in which law formation is a continual round, should never, simply for the sake of convenience, cross the street against a no-walk sign. Freedom to disobey when it matters can exist only if at all other times perfect obedience is yielded. For disobedience is attended by the overhanging threat of anarchy. We did not ration ourselves in disobedience, and those in authority in the universities in the late sixties imposed no rationing. Coming as the third wave of massive disobedience movements in fifteen years, the demonstrations of the late sixties, including the most peaceable and legitimate ones of all, carried the clear and present danger of anarchy.

The point may be put in another and more general way with reference not only to civil disobedience. In 1969, President Kingman Brewster of Yale invited a number of speakers about to appear at a Yale alumni seminar to address the subject, "What is happening to morality today?" My answer at the time was: "It threatens to engulf us." The legal order has heaved and groaned for years under a prodigality of moral causes and, if not broken, it is no wonder that it is badly bent. Vietnam, let us not forget, was not only a moral error but, for its authors, a moral urgency. The urgencies of "peace with honor," of the clean life, of patriotism—in a word, Watergate—were merely the last straws. It is ironic, but entirely natural, that "law-and-order" as a moral imperative should have clashed with the legal order. For the legal order, after all, is an accommodation. It cannot sustain the continuous assault of moral imperatives, not even the moral imperative of "law-and-order," which as a moral imperative has only a verbal resemblance to the ends of the legal order. No legal order can sustain such a bombardment, and the less so a federal constitutional order of separated and diffused powers. It is the premise of our legal order that its own complicated arrangements, although subject to evolutionary change, are more important than any momentary objective. This premise must give way at times to accommodate inevitable change. Change which is significant, as Justice Brandeis once wrote, manifests itself more "in intellectual and moral conceptions than in material things." But our legal order cannot endure too rapid a pace of change in moral conceptions, and its fundamental premise is that its own stability is itself a high moral value, in most circumstances the highest. The legal order must be given time to absorb change, to accommodate it to itself as well as itself to it. If the pace is forced, there can be no law.

The assault upon the legal order by moral imperatives was not only or perhaps even most effectively an assault from the outside. As I have suggested, it came as well from within, in the Supreme Court headed for fifteen years by Earl Warren. When a lawyer stood before him arguing his side of a case on the basis of some legal doctrine or other, or making a procedural point, or contending that the Constitution allocated competence over a given issue to another branch of government than the Supreme Court or to the states rather than to the federal government, the chief justice would shake him off saying, "Yes, yes, yes, but is it [whatever the case exemplified about law or about the society], is it *right*? Is it *good*?" More than once, and in some of its most important actions, the Warren Court got over doctrinal difficulties or issues of the allocation of competences among various institutions by asking what it viewed as a decisive practical question: If the Court did not take a certain action which was *right* and *good*, would other institutions do so, given political realities? The Warren Court took the greatest pride in cutting through legal technicalities, in piercing through procedure to substance. But legal technicalities are the stuff of law, and piercing through a particular substance to get to procedures suitable to many substances is in fact what the task of law most often is.

The derogators of procedure and of technicalities, and other anti-institutional forces who rode high, on the bench as well as off, were the armies of conscience and of ideology. If it is paradoxical that they were also the armies of a new populism it is not a paradox to wonder at, for it has occurred often before, not least of all in Rousseau, who may be counted the patron philosopher of the time. The paradox is that the people whom the populist exalts may well—will frequently—not vote for the results that conscience and ideology dictate. But then one can always hope, or identify the general will with the people despite their votes, and let the Supreme Court bespeak the people's general will when the vote comes out wrong. There was a powerful strain of populism in the rhetoric by which the Court supported its one-man, one-vote doctrine, and after promulgating it the Court strove mightily to strike down all barriers—not only the poll tax, but duration of residence, all manner of special qualifications, and even in some measure, age—to the enlargement and true universalization of the franchise. In this the Court led successfully. It became irresistible dogma that no qualification for voting made any sense. It did not matter that you were a transient—and wherever the election catches you, you vote with no questions asked. No connection to place is relevant, there is no room for balancing interests and places, no need to structure institutions so that they might rest on different electoral foundations and in the aggregate be better able to generate consent. Every impediment, every distortion, including the electoral college, must go. All that matters is the people, told by the head.

Here the connection with attitudes that at least contributed to Watergate is direct. It was utterly inevitable that such a populist fixation should tend toward the concentration of power in that single institution which has the most immediate link to the largest constituency. Naturally the consequence was a Gaullist presidency, making war, making peace, spending, saving, being secret, being open, doing what is necessary, and needing no excuse for aggregating power to itself besides the excuse that it could do more effectively what other institutions, particularly Congress, did not do very rapidly or very well, or under particular political circumstances would not do at all. This was a leaf from the Warren Court's book, but the presidency could undertake to act anti-institutionally in this fashion with more justification because, unlike the Court, it could claim not only a constituency but the largest one. This presidency acknowledged accountability only at quadrennial plebiscites, but not to other, less plebiscitary institutions, and certainly not to irresponsible private ones, or to something called "public opinion," which is led and formed in mysterious ways, rather than being told by the head. The accumulation of power in the presidency did not begin with Richard M. Nixon, of course, but it reached heights made possible by the populism of the day. There was a time there, soon after the election of 1972, when Mr. Nixon gave the impression that he thought the American political process had taken place, so to speak, that it was over for a while, and that he could simply rule. We know again now that an election is the beginning as well as the culmination of a political process, and that the president, separate, independent, and critically important as he is, is part of the process, not its ruler. We were being led to forget, however, and had it not been for Watergate, conceivably we might have forgotten.

The presidency of inherent powers, futurism, populism, and certainly moral urgency—these have too often been the vestments of liberalism in this century, though worn for the most part with a certain modesty. Diffusion of power, pragmatism, the relativism of values, gradualism, institutionalism, process, procedure, legality, technicalities—these were allowed to become the cloak of conservatism, indeed of reaction. Well, the cloak was not wanted in the White House either. I don't know when Mr. Nixon caught the liberals bathing, but he did walk off with their clothes and stood forth wearing the plebiscitary presidency, his own futurism, and his own moral imperatives. We are all liberals, we are all conservatives, Mr. Nixon might have said.

Watergate was the latest assault, the only one which was at once vicious and powerful, the latest assault in an age of assaultive politics. We cannot survive a politics of moral attack. We must resume the politics of Burke's computing principle. The denominations to be computed are very often moral, to be sure, but few if any are absolute, few if any imperative. And the highest morality almost always is the morality of process.

5

Moral Authority
and the Intellectual

5

Moral Authority
and the Intellectual

Although the furor of the campuses in the late 1960s has been succeeded by peace—at any rate by external peace—the conditions of emergency and crisis still prevail for the university and for the intellectual, even if in ways less obvious than before. It behooves us, therefore, to reexamine the very foundations of our conduct. For they have been questioned, radically and violently. We have been charged with moral neutrality, with gradualism, with betrayal of moral imperatives.

Now our universities have, by and large with good cause but not without difficulty, been persuaded to the belief that knowledge and insight, like art, are the products of independent minds following each its own bent, and are not often to be attained otherwise. In universities, professionals of many disciplines can follow lines of inquiry determined by themselves, individually and collegially, and dictated by no one else, on grounds either ideological or practical. While not all universities or colleges pretend to be such places, and other institutions like research institutes can be, only in a university can inquiry and teaching constitute one creative whole, so that the knowledge and insight of the scholar and the methods by which he gained them are shared with the student; so that the student may be the scholar's company, nourishing him, giving as well as taking, in a word, collaborating. To this end, teachers must be free to teach, as free in their teaching as in their scholarship; and the enterprise—with its twin freedoms of inquiry and of teaching—must be judged by professional criteria and none other. No one will claim that the ideal university exists, or that all members of all faculties are intent on independent intel-

127

lectual labors, but we approach no closer to the ideal by admitting nonprofessional and nonintellectual criteria.

The young, like society at large, have their own perceptions of their needs, and society has an instrument at its disposal for bringing these needs home; it is the market, inside the university and out, and in the aggregate, over time, it is quite effective. Students vote with their feet, choosing the university they prefer and accepting or rejecting parts of the elective curriculum; their parents vote with their pocketbooks. The curriculum of every university is witness to that. The market serves as a limit on academic freedom.

While, like many other institutions, universities are sluggish in times of rapid change, the university as the practical servant of the society can all too readily swallow up the university as the haven of independent inquiry. It would do so, to the ultimate detriment of the society itself, if students were given a decisive voice in setting the curriculum, or otherwise in directing the university's intellectual life, just as if alumni, or government, or churches, or labor unions, or business, or professional associations were given such a voice. Some universities may well be miseducating students or educating them insufficiently, but nothing in the experience of the recent years with students acting en masse indicates that they know how to do things better. The mood of many students is anti-intellectual, anti-professional. They do not want to know, they would rather feel and be. Is it seriously contended that they should be allowed to feel and be and to not know, in a university which then certifies them as knowing enough to commit surgery on a person, architecture on a building, or a law suit on a client? However embarrassingly unfashionable it may be to insist on power and privilege, inroads on the autonomy of faculties are inroads on academic freedom; the abandonment of any faculty control over appointments, curriculum, and academic standards is the abandonment of the ends of the university.

But the ends of the university, we academics have been told, and the methods and structures designed to attain them are political and, we have been told, our ends and our methods are wrong politically, or at least unacceptable or undesirable. A different set of political objectives and means must—by means themselves political—be substituted for those we have avowed and practiced. It may be admitted that the university is, by extension, politically involved. The university is committed to freedom of inquiry, to the method of reason, however fallible. It is agnostic, and it is neutral to a degree, and from certain vantage points, reason, agnosticism, and neutrality can be seen as political. To the radical—of the Left or of the Right—intent on the attainment of immediate social ends which he conceives as moral imperatives, such neutrality appears as a commitment to the other side. Neutrality and agnosticism are, indeed, likely in practice to result in an attitude of gradualism and a rejection of absolute activism. Intellectuals *are* committed, in short, to thought without action, and to thought which may oppose action and it may as well be conceded that a neutrality proceeding from such a commitment does have practical consequences. Not for nothing did the Nazi say, "When I hear the word culture, I reach for my revolver." A brilliant young radical writer in the United States a few years ago echoed the Maoist view, saying "Morality"—and he could as well have added reason, too—"is what comes out of the barrel of a gun."

There is an analogy between the agnosticism and neutrality of the university and the agnosticism and neutrality of the free, secular public school or of courts of law. The public school does not appear neutral to people who believe that primary education ought to have a moral content, based on the revealed truth of religion. And the essence of the law is a lack of political involvement; it bespeaks neutrality, yet also the deepest sort of commitment to the judicial process and to the process of law—deliberate, gradual, consensual, responsive ultimately, and if only indirectly, to majorities but not to plebiscites, and limited as to means. This is a commitment to a political position.

Universities and professional and scholarly organizations are also institutions of the existing order, but special institutions with special functions, including the questioning of their own and others' premises and those of the society itself and the entertaining of ideas subversive of the society. Yet, as institutions of the existing order and supported by it, they have an implicit bias toward its basic presuppositions, an implicit allegiance to the minimal principles and structures that tend toward its preservation. This also is a political bias. Judges do not take an oath to humanity at large, or swear to follow their own consciences; they take an oath to support the law, and in the United States, the Constitution, with its own political meaning. Universities are less explicitly committed, and private universities not at all. Still, all institutions which require substantial support from the society—even the universities—must realistically be viewed as resting on an assumption of generalized allegiance to that society. Even a university's unlimited freedom of inquiry and freedom of radical opinion assure institutional acceptance of the legitimacy of the regime. Political involvement in these extended senses of the term is as defensible as it is ineluctable, and it is fully consistent with freedom of inquiry.

But, more recently, a measure of ideological, political commitment, an active engagement with immediate social and economic problems, has been asked of universities. What would the consequence of such passionate and practical political commitment be to the freedom of inquiry that is the heart of the university? A legislator or judge is expected to take individual positions, his votes are recorded and publicized, and he is nowhere identified automatically with the positions of his institution. But the population of a university—student, faculty, and other—is too large to permit such separate identity. It is difficult to see how an economist who thinks minimum wage laws foolish and bad can maintain his identity in an institution that favors minimum wage laws, or how a non-Marxist can maintain his identity in a Marxist institution. If universities as institutions are to be identified politically, faculty and students would sort themselves out on political grounds, and the institutions would then become monolithic. An institution politically involved in this sense could hardly avoid committing its largely human resources to that end; it would try to induce and finally to compel its members to devote themselves to the attainment of the end to which the institution is committed. That is the death not merely of diversity and exchange of ideas, but of free inquiry altogether. In the last analysis, what else can be intended by demands for political involvement and, even if not intended, how can it be avoided? Loss of intellectual quality, and ultimately of content, would follow.

Tillman Durdin reported from Hongkong in the *New York Times* on September 25, 1970, on the reopening—after years of cultural revolution—of Chinese universities, that

> The admission process . . . of the universities [has] been radically revised according to directives of Mao Tse-tung, putting class background ahead of academic achievement. . . . Students were selected as meritorious workers, soldiers and peasants after repeated discussion among the masses.
>
> Many of those selected . . . have meager intellectual qualifications but rate highly in proletarian credentials.[1]

Later, in 1973, Mr. Durdin, and a visiting Australian-American academic, Professor Ross Terrill, reported some backsliding in Chinese universities, but it was mostly covert and it was only backsliding. Here and there, college entrance examinations covering intellectual subject-matter had reappeared, though not under their proper and despised name; they were called, instead, with touching disingenuousness, "investigations of cultural knowledge," and if an applicant was rejected because he had failed the "investigation," the university had to explain and justify its rejection.[2]

Without suggesting too close an analogy to the Chinese experience, this is the logical place to note that American universities have been subjected, and many have in varying measures succumbed, to political pressures for the dilution and even the abandonment of intellectual standards in the recruitment of faculty and students from certain minority groups, including women, who are assuredly no minority in the population at large. The problem is complex. The groups in question have certainly been disadvantaged in the past, and an effort to recruit them and to open opportunities to them is overdue. Moreover, our admissions tests

1. *New York Times*, September 25, 1970, p. 10.
2. Ibid., August 13, 1973, p. 5; August 27, 1973, p. 6.

are sometimes tests not of capacity only, not even sure indicators
of performance in the university environment, but, in the words of
the Chinese euphemism, "investigations of cultural knowledge,"
class-bound and framed in terms of the culture of a dominant
group, not the culture in a large sense. To the extent that this is
true we test not merely for capacity but for a background which
may not be relevant to capacity, and candidates may fail not for
lack of relevant capacity but for lack of irrelevant background.
Culture in a larger sense is what universities aim to transmit and
what students must work and achieve in, but parochial standards
within it should be transcended. Instead, we have often yielded to
pressures simply to relax standards. This political concession is
wrong.

The dilution of standards in the university as a whole, adminis-
trators and faculties have told themselves, is not serious if the
number recruited as faculty and students is kept low in propor-
tion to total numbers. The solution, in other words, is the quota,
the *numerus clausus*, by whatever name it may be called or by
whatever euphemism disguised. But the cost to the university
and to the society is serious. There is a cost in loss of efficiency and
productivity—in the university immediately and in business and
the professions later on—from which no one benefits. And there
is a cost in injustice. A quota is a two-edged device: for every one
it includes it cuts someone else out, and we are not wise enough to
administer the exclusions justly, even assuming the justice and
wisdom of our inclusions, which I do not.[3]

"Circumstances," wrote Burke, "(which with some gentlemen
pass for nothing) give in reality to every political principle its
distinguishing color and discriminating effect. The circumstances
are what render every civil and political scheme beneficial or
noxious to mankind." So in the case of affirmative action on equal
opportunity. If the Constitution prohibits exclusion of blacks and
other minorities on racial grounds, it cannot permit the exclusion
of whites on similar grounds; for it must be the exclusion on racial

3. The author and Philip Kurland were attorneys for the Anti-
Defamation League of B'nai B'rith, amicus curiae in DeFunis v. Ode-
gaard, 416 U.S. 312 (1974).

grounds which offends the Constitution, and not the particular skin color of the person excluded.

The lesson of the great decisions of the Supreme Court and the lesson of contemporary history have been the same for at least a generation: discrimination on the basis of race is illegal, immoral, unconstitutional, inherently wrong, and destructive of democratic society. Now this is to be unlearned and we are told that this is not a matter of fundamental principle but only a matter of whose ox is gored. Those for whom racial equality was demanded are to be more equal than others. Having found support in the Constitution for equality, they now claim support for inequality under the same Constitution. Yet a racial quota derogates the human dignity and individuality of all to whom it is applied; it is invidious in principle as well as in practice. Moreover, it can as easily be turned against those it purports to help. The history of the racial quota is a history of subjugation, not beneficence. Its evil lies not in its name but in its effect; a quota is a divider of society, a creator of castes, and it is all the worse for its racial base, especially in a society desperately striving for an equality that will make race irrelevant.

The cost in efficiency, as well as the injustice, ought to be deemed unacceptable. Productivity and efficiency are on the decline anyway in this country, quite seriously in some sectors of the economy. Accepting further deterioration is no help to anyone, not merely in the very long run but in a much shorter run. And in a society in which men expect to succeed by hard work and to better themselves by making themselves better, a society, moreover, in which prejudice for some groups has only recently been overcome so that the expectation has begun to be fully met, it is no trivial moral wrong to proceed systematically to defeat it. In many employments artificial qualifications have been erected, or wrong ones, unduly bound to middle-class culture and insufficiently related to true efficiency, and these can properly be reexamined. But to reject an applicant to a university faculty or for a position in business or for a job as an electrician or in the civil service who has met established, realistic, and unchanged qualifications in favor of a less qualified candidate is morally wrong and

in the aggregate disastrous. Where the casting of a wider recruitment net produces no results, our energies ought to go into
training and tutoring the disadvantaged and the excluded, not into
compromising and ruining, morally and practically, the society
that has wronged them in the past, as it earlier wronged others,
and which now recognizes their just complaint.

Standards and their impersonal application—free of group as
well as personal prejudices—guard us against our inevitable
tendency to injustice, I would say our human appetite for injustice.
Man is born to injustice in another sense, no doubt, divine injustice, the injustice of unequally distributed endowments. I think
the teaching of our tradition is that the only way to avoid adding
the crueler injustice of man himself to that of the cosmos is to
accept the latter in its irreducible form.

There is an additional cost of politicizing the university by
pressing on it commitments and missions. I approach this point
with caution, because the university is not a church, its members
are no priesthood, they are not even any sort of a political elite
with judgment on affairs that is particularly acute and worth heed-
ing. On the whole, I think the contrary is true. And yet, though
no priests or philosopher kings, scholars often bring a valuable
detachment to affairs. All too little information and opinion enter the universe of political discourse with the credit that
attaches to disinterestedness. Much of what there is comes from
academic and professional persons, whose credentials are certified by universities or other professional and scholarly organizations, and are known to be certified in accordance with neutral
standards, not political objectives. Persons so certified then speak
with a certain moral authority; they inject into the political
process something the process cannot easily generate itself—
dispassionate, informed, disinterested judgment, which looks
beyond the interests and objectives immediately engaged in the
debate. If the "accrediting" institutions themselves become politically engaged, their accreditation loses its value, and society
will be the poorer. Disinterested judgment will have lost much of
its moral authority.

It is as if judges were assumed to decide on the basis of personal predilection, class interest, or political affiliation. No one of course can step altogether out of himself, but there is a category of men, including judges, to whom we assign the role of making the effort. Some maintain that this is a sham, that no one really plays such a role, and if that were so it would be as well to be candid about it. For those who believe that it is a sham, political involvement on the part of universities and like organizations is a matter of candor. But in truth, the role can be played and is a valuable one, and if that is so, then for universities political involvement constitutes a wanton abandonment of it. Such consequences, to be sure, come only gradually. If a university's board of trustees or a faculty votes by a preponderant majority to commit itself to one or another political cause, nothing fundamental probably occurs. The effect is cumulative. The consequences follow over time from many actions in the aggregate. Hence it has been urged that a faculty or a board of trustees or the annual meeting of a professional association can permit itself to vote on a critical issue of fundamental moral importance, an issue of the sort that does not arise every other day—for example, the Vietnam war. Issues of seemingly fundamental moral importance do not arise every other day for everyone; still, they arise every day for someone. And each time it will have to be a majority which decides the jurisdictional issue, as well as the substantive one, which decides whether an issue is of such fundamental moral importance as to call for taking a position, and what that position should be. Within the confines of any culture, one may concede, some rare ultimate issues would almost universally be viewed as of overriding moral significance. Even then, all the institution can do that individuals cannot is in some sense to put its function on the line, to close its doors or something of the sort, or else over the longer run, to commit its resources. But is enough gained by that? If exceptions are conceded on certain issues of the greatest magnitude, the danger of sliding into a continuous course of political involvement is all too great.

The Scranton Commission, appointed by President Nixon in 1970 to study the causes of student unrest, enjoined universities to "remain politically neutral, except in those rare cases in which

their own integrity, educational purpose or preservation are at
stake." Perhaps it brings us back to the notion that universities
are after all committed to a set of basic values and processes, and
when those values and processes are in question they should act
in their defense. The commitment among other things is to political neutrality. The Scranton Commission was saying that political
involvement is justified only when necessary to avoid it. And this
is the sort of political involvement that the German universities
in the 1930s failed to undertake. They did not resist being pushed
into political involvement. That was their sin. We in the universities have been urged to sin in quite the opposite direction.

And where has this temptation to sin led us in the university
and beyond? Where could it lead us still? It led us during the
tumultuous 1960s and into 1970, on the campuses, to threats of
violence and actual violence. On April 23, 1970, the faculty of
Yale College met, and having heard the president of the university
express his skepticism that black revolutionaries could get a fair
trial anywhere in the United States, voted to countenance a student
strike protesting the trial of Bobby Seale and several other Black
Panthers on a charge of murder. I was at the meeting and so
voted, and did not really feel ashamed until I walked out through
the crowd of students who we had known were out there, whom
we had heard, and who now cheered us. Most faculty and many
students continued to attend class, and there was little attempt
to bring pressure on them. Nothing we could have done probably
would have dispelled the hysteria of passion that had taken hold
and many things we might have done would have heightened the
dangerous threat to the college and the town. But there *is* cause to
be ashamed. We did not return a rational answer to our students,
because we were too alone and it was too late. If we had said what
is true, that the trial was no crisis, that it was inconceivable not to
let it proceed, and that there is no reason to equate the police in
Chicago with the courts in New Haven and with the state and
federal courts that sit to correct the errors of courts in New Haven;
and if we had added that the university would continue to function, if we had said all that we would have been denounced as
rigid, unresponsive, authoritarian; we would have risked riots and

destruction, and been saddled with responsibility for possible police overreaction. That is what it had come to: truth and the function of the university are irrelevant and dangerous. We had listened—quietly, even solemnly, as if it were rational—to incredibly loose talk about the obsolescence and rottenness of our society and all our institutions, and came to parrot it in order to propitiate a sizable number of young.

It all started with the Vietnam war, which did represent a malfunction of the system; the continuation of an insufferable war led quite naturally and reasonably to talk of systemic crisis. Among academics and other intellectuals, let alone "poets, yeggs and thirsties," it became not merely fashionable, but required, to speak apocalyptically of such systemic crisis. The war had to stop, the march into Cambodia was a gruesome error, the cities are a mess, our rivers and our air smell awful, and the blacks will not and ought not stand for being forgotten again. The talk of apocalypse became relatively muted only to grow in volume with Watergate. Watergate, it was said, proves irrefutably that the system is a hoax and must be torn down. But there is another crisis that could incapacitate us from dealing with these. It is the crisis of the abandonment of reason, of standards, of measure, the loss of balance and judgment. Among its symptoms were the incivility and even violence of rhetoric and action that academics and other intellectuals domesticated into their universe of discourse, and the interdiction of objective discussion that they increasingly tolerated, an incivility and violence and interdiction happily on the decline on the campus but unfortunately not altogether abandoned.

It is not reasonable to extend a systemic indictment to the entire structure of government, to the electoral process itself, to the administration of justice, to every debatable action that a new national administration thinks it has a mandate to take, and to every type of institution. Everything can be improved, even radically improved, and change is the law of life. But not everything can be improved instantly, and not all change is good. And destructive nihilism is evil no matter how motivated. These things it has been unfashionable for intellectuals and their audiences to say and hear. In New Haven, where the peace was kept in 1970, the university was full of painted and stenciled slogans and threats called dissent—but in truth vandalism, a kind of aggression almost physical, in content most often a series of curses without pretense of an effort to persuade. No principle of a free society requires institutions public or private to allow such verbal violence within their precincts, and to permit reasoned analysis to be driven out while passionate assertion is assumed to be presumptively right, and dispassionate judgment presumptively immoral. Yet we have observed it and listened to it respectfully, and thus have legitimated it. Because the university, the government, and the legal order—we heard it said and assented to—are thoroughly unworthy, they may not use force to protect themselves against violence, but force may justly be used against them.

The young were right about the war in Indochina. The young are right too about a great deal of racism and about the debasement of values by commercialism. But many are wrong about repression. The society is free and open, if flawed and gravely troubled. Watergate revealed corruption and conspiracy; it also revealed that the country's institutions were strong enough to hold the corrupt to account. Our domestic problems can be solved or alleviated only through the democratic political process, which is slow and prone to error.

But revolution would produce only something less responsive to claims of social justice and infinitely more coercive and oppressive. Of course, the objective situation in the United States, as Marxists would say, is such that violent repression is more likely than violent revolution. A revolutionary frame of mind is dangerous not only because it may evoke an effective counter-revolution; it is dangerous also, the more dangerous, because guilt-ridden and otherwise disoriented liberals and intellectuals are intimidated by it into damaging the institutions that hold out the only realistic hope for the redress of many legitimate grievances, and that alone stand in the way of counter-revolution. It is probably statable in the form of an equation that so many rampages, so many bricks and bottles thrown, and even so many epithets hurled will eventually produce so many innocent victims; and also that so much talk of the rottenness of men and institutions, solemnly countenanced by so many apparently rational people, will produce so much incendiary counter-rhetoric and counter-rampaging. A price is inevitably paid for destroying the order of society. If the streets belong to the people, they are going to belong to all the people, not just young radicals. Self-righteousness and zealotry are human attributes, not political positions. If they are tolerated on the left, they will gain ascendancy on the right. "Kings," wrote Burke, "will be tyrants from policy, when subjects are rebels from principle."

Liberals who want no revolution are forever trying to appease the revolutionaries in order to entice them back up on the raft. If the Committee for Public Justice, organized by numerous distinguished lawyers and academics in 1970, was right in its charge that the Bill of Rights is "being killed," we need, of course, to listen more seriously and with less shock to proposals for scrapping the whole system. We need to be open to radical programs of protest, even if they do portend violence. For violence, applied intelligently and as humanely as possible, does not necessarily discredit a quest for human rights when these are trampled underfoot, and are about to be snuffed out by concerted repression. Extremism in the defense of liberty is no vice, except one has doubts about the kind of liberty the maker of that phrase was defending. If, on the other hand, it is not true but simply another instance of rhetorical inflation, we need to ask whether announcing the imminent death of our rights may not help to bring it about.

The moral authority of liberalism is lost when the fundamental principles and attitudes of liberalism are compromised or abandoned, for these principles are the essence of the American political tradition. They touch Lincoln's mystic chords of memory. They are the foundation of the liberal ascendancy in our politics. The danger is not that the moral authority of liberalism will be destroyed, thus bringing on rule by the Right, but that the moral authority of liberalism will thus bring on the revolution of the Left, if not its rule. This danger is not a trifling one. The country, the revolutionary Left has said, is brutal, inhuman, racist, self-destructive. The society is debased, hopeless, beyond repair. If that is true, only the pacifists among masses of people who share allegiance to liberal principles would long continue to resist the revolutionary idea. And most of us who waged World War II and called for the use of troops to secure civil rights in the South are not pacifists, and neither are our children. It is therefore no light thing for spokesmen of the liberal tradition to infest political discourse with a pestilence of condemnations of this imperfect but not quite debased society.

Ills there are in our society, as the revolutionaries have reminded us. And there is no point in a recital of achievements. All that can be proved is that we are entitled to high hopes. Yet revolutions are born of hope, not of despair, even though they need the rhetoric of despair to justify the dirty work by which they are made. The question about a revolution, therefore, is not what has it despaired of, but what are its hopes? Our recent revolutionists have offered us hatred. They despise and dehumanize the persons, and they condemn the concerns and the aspirations, of the vast majority of their countrymen. They have offered for the future, so far as their spokesmen have been able to make clear, the Maypole dance and, in considerable tension if not contradiction, a vision of "liberated" masses adjuring profit, competition, personal achievement, and any form of gratification not instantly and equally available to all. A pamphlet issued by the Yippies urged the young:

> Burn your money. You know life is a dream and all our institutions are man-made illusions, effective only because you take the dream for reality. Break down the family, church, nation, city, economy, turn life into an art form and theater of the soul. What is needed is a generation of people who are freaky, crazy, irrational, sexy, angry, irreligious, childish, and mad . . . who lure the youth with music, pot, and acid . . . who redefine the normal. . . . Burn your houses down and you will be free.[4]

4. Quoted in Jason Epstein, *The Great Conspiracy Trial* (New York: Random House, 1970), p. 310.

Suppose millions upon millions of us cannot be persuaded that we would be happier if we freed ourselves of the achievement ethic, or happier traipsing over a green hill than swilling beer in front of the TV, have those seized of a higher vision the right to coerce us into conforming to it? Never mind that the vision is anti-intellectual, that mind and art are to be leveled, that the spirit will suffocate. How will we maintain material conditions, let alone improve them, if we abandon the miserable, debased production of goods which now obsesses us? Who will mind the store while we dance in the streets?

In the end perhaps the revolutionaries will unmask themselves. The faith embodied in the First Amendment is not only that in a free society few will want to make a revolution, but that where the revolutionary idea may be freely ventilated it will defeat itself. The answers are obvious: those of us who insist on striving and on swilling beer don't really know what we want, and the revolution would enable us freely to want what we should. And we would not be dancing in the streets all the time but fulfilling ourselves at play and at work. Those of us who play too much would be told gently, persuasively, but in the end firmly by our new leaders (positioned not above us, but side-by-side with us) that for our own and the common good we ought to work more and play less. And we would do it gladly, for the society would be ours, not the CIA's, as it is now. When we work, we will do the work that fulfills us, not some task to which we have been arbitrarily assigned, and if we fall into some individual error about what work really does fulfill us, we will be shown our mistake, we will see it, and proceed to do what we ought to do. It all rings true. Such a system can surely be built. It is only that there is a name for the means that must be employed to create that system and maintain it. That name is tyranny. Our freedom, as Holmes said of judges, may be more molecular than molar, and it is more political than personal. But we would all recognize tyranny when we saw it.

When bushels of desires and objectives are conceived as moral imperatives, it is natural to seek their achievement by any means. There is no need to fear that the same means will be open to others, because the objectives of those others will be understood to be bad and unacceptable whatever the means used to attain them. One has to believe rather that no amount of opinion can be eternally certain of the moral rightness of its preferences, and that whoever is in power in government is entitled to give effect to his preferences. Then, but only then, it is crucial that everyone adhere to certain procedures, and that some means be forbidden to all. The fabric is held together by agreement on means, which are equally available or foreclosed to all, and by allegiance to a limited number of broad first principles concerning the ends of government. These first principles are what the law of the Constitution is about. They change over time and develop, and become entrenched as they gather common assent. Beyond them lies policy, and there lie our differences.

If most of the things that politics is about are not seen as existing well this side of moral imperatives, in a middle distance, if they are not seen as subject on both sides of a division of opinion to fallible human choice, then the only thing left to a society is to succumb to or be seized by a dictatorship of the self-righteous. I do not wish to overstate the case, but this seems to me inevitably the conclusion to which disenchanted and embittered simplifiers and moralizers must come. But if we do resist the seductive temptations of moral imperatives and fix our eye on that middle distance where values are provisionally held, are tested, and evolve within the legal order—derived from the morality of process, which is the morality of consent—our moral authority will carry more weight. The computing principle Burke urged upon us can lead us then to an imperfect justice, for there is no other kind.

The Writings of
Alexander Mordecai Bickel

Books

The Unpublished Opinions of Mr. Justice Brandeis (1957).

The Least Dangerous Branch: The Supreme Court at the Bar of Politics (1963).

Politics and the Warren Court (1965).

The New Age of Political Reform: The Electoral College, the Convention, and the Party System (1968).

The Supreme Court and the Idea of Progress (1970).

Reform and Continuity: The Electoral College, the Convention, and the Party System (1971).

The Caseload of the Supreme Court and What, If Anything, to Do About It (1973).

The Morality of Consent (1975).

The Judiciary and Responsible Government 1910–1921 (Holmes Devise History of the U.S. Supreme Court, to be published).

Articles in Legal Periodicals and in Books

Doctrine of Forum Non Coveniens As Applied in Federal Courts in Matters of Admiralty, *35 Cornell L.Q. 12* (1949).

Judge and Jury—Inconsistent Verdicts in the Federal Courts, *63 Harv. L. Rev. 649* (1950).

The Original Understanding and the Segregation Decision, *69 Harv. L. Rev. 1* (1955), reprinted in *Selected Essays on Constitutional Law* (Ass'n. Am. Law Schools ed. 1963).

Strathearn S.S. Co. v. Dillon—An Unpublished Opinion by Mr. Justice Brandeis, *69 Harv. L. Rev. 1177* (1956).

Legislative Purpose and the Judicial Process: The Lincoln Mills Case, *71 Harv. L. Rev.* (1957) (with H. Wellington).

The Supreme Court, 1960, Term—Foreword: The Passive Virtues, *75 Harv. L. Rev. 40* (1961), reprinted in *Selected Essays on Constitutional Law* (Ass'n. Am. Law Schools ed. 1963).

The Durability of Colegrove v. Green, *72 Yale L.J. 39* (1962).

A Panel: The Proper Role of the United States Supreme Court in Civil Liberties Cases, *10 Wayne L. Rev. 473* (1964) (with D. Dorsen, P. Bator, C. Foote & C. Reich).

Applied Politics and the Science of Law: Writings of the Harvard Period, in *Felix Frankfurter: A Tribute* (W. Mendelson ed. 1964).

The Decade of School Desegregation: Progress and Prospects, *64 Colum. L. Rev. 193* (1964).

The Meaning of the Civil Rights Act, in *Civil Rights* (G. McClellan ed. 1964).

Discrimination in Education, in *Discrimination and the Law* (V. Countryman ed. 1965).

Felix Frankfurter, *78 Harv. L. Rev. 1527* (1965).

Judicial Review of Police Methods in Law Enforcement: The Role of the Supreme Court of the United States, *44 Texas L. Rev. 954* (1966).

Symposium: Southern Justice: Justice and Compassion, *37 Miss L.J. 396* (1966) (with W. Ethridge, Jr., J. Patterson, W. Walter, S. Luckett & J. Doyle III).

The Voting Rights Cases, *1966 Sup. Ct. Rev. 79.*

Supreme Court and Political Democracy, *44 F.R.D. 158* (1968).

Mr. Taft Rehabilitates the Court, *79 Yale L.J. 1* (1969).

Congress, the President and the Power to Wage War, *48 Chi.-Kent L. Rev. 131* (1971).

The New Supreme Court: Prospects and Problems, *45 Tul. L. Rev. 229* (1971).

Commentary, in *A. Rosenthal, Federal Regulation of Campaign Finance: Some Constitutional Questions* (1972).

Citizenship in the American Constitution, *15 Ariz. L. Rev. 369* (1973).

Civil Disobedience and the Duty to Obey, *8 Gonz. L. Rev. 199* (1973).

Commentary, in *Watergate, Politics, and the Legal Process* (Am. Enterprise Inst. Round Table 1974).

Articles in *The New Republic*

Chief Justice Warren and the Presidency, *New Republic*, Jan. 23, 1956, at 8.

Ninety-six Congressmen versus the Nine Justices, *New Republic*, Apr. 23, 1956, at 11.

Integration: The Second Year in Perspective, *New Republic*, Oct. 8, 1956, at 12.

Passion and Patience, *New Republic*, Nov. 12, 1956, at 15.

On the Retirement of Justice Reed, *New Republic*, Mar. 4, 1957, at 6.

Eisenhower, Faubus, and the Court, *New Republic*, Sept. 30, 1957, at 5.

The Hearts of Man, *New Republic*, Oct. 7, 1957, at 6.

A Communication: "Paths to Desegregation by Prof. Charles L. Black, Jr.," *New Republic*, Nov. 4, 1957, at 3 (letter).

Brownell's Departure, *New Republic*, Nov. 11, 1957, at 6.

Mr. Justice Frankfurter at Seventy-Six, *New Republic*, Nov. 18, 1957, at 7.

Judicial Restraint and the Bill of Rights, *New Republic*, May 12, 1958, at 16.

Inexplicable Document, *New Republic*, Sept. 29, 1958, at 9.

Law and Reason, *New Republic*, Nov. 3, 1958, at 18.

Congressional Review of Passport Policy, *New Republic*, Dec. 29, 1958, at 9.

Court-Curbing Time, *New Republic*, May 25, 1959, at 10.

Justices on Display, *New Republic*, Sept. 14, 1959, at 20.

Mr. Justice Black, *New Republic*, Mar. 14, 1960, at 13.

What the Founders Believed, *New Republic*, July 18, 1960, at 15.

Next President and Civil Rights, *New Republic*, Oct. 13, 1960, at 17.

Robert F. Kennedy: The Case against Him for Attorney General, *New Republic*, Jan. 9, 1961, at 15.

Philosophy of a Legal Realist, *New Republic*, Apr. 24, 1961, at 30.

Communist Cases, *New Republic*, June 19, 1961, at 15.

Integration—The Seven Lean Years, *New Republic*, Sept. 25, 1961, at 17.

Portrait of Justice Holmes, *New Republic*, Nov. 6, 1961, at 19.

Democracy and the Private Citizen, *New Republic*, Feb. 5, 1962, at 22.

The Great Apportionment Case, *New Republic*, Apr. 9, 1962, at 13.

Civil Rights: The Kennedy Record, *New Republic*, Dec. 15, 1962, at 11.

The New Court, *New Republic*, Mar. 16, 1963, at 15.

Crime and Reapportionment, *New Republic*, Apr. 6, 1963, at 5.

Civil Rights Boil-Up, *New Republic*, June 8, 1963, at 10.

Civil Rights Act of 1963, *New Republic*, July 6, 1963, at 9.

Civil Rights and the Congress, *New Republic*, Aug. 3, 1963, at 14.

Civil Rights as Amended, *New Republic*, Nov. 16, 1963, at 7.

Liberals and Civil Rights, *New Republic*, Dec. 28, 1963, at 9.

Beyond Tokenism, *New Republic*, Jan. 4, 1964, at 11.

Sleepers in the Civil Rights Bill, *New Republic*, Feb. 29, 1964, at 14.

The Court Intervenes, *New Republic*, Mar. 14, 1964, at 28; Feb. 29, 1964, at 5.

Bobby Baker's Silence: Back to the Fifth, *New Republic*, Mar. 21, 1964, at 9.

After a Civil Rights Act, *New Republic*, May 9, 1964, at 11.

Integrated Cohabitation, *New Republic*, May 30, 1964, at 4.

Reapportionment and the Courts, *New Republic*, June 27, 1964, at 7.

Supreme Court Fissures: Seeds of Discord in the New Majority, *New Republic*, July 11, 1964, at 15.

Battle over Brandeis, *New Republic*, Aug. 8, 1964, at 25.

Barry Fights the Court, *New Republic*, Oct. 10, 1964, at 9.

Justice and the Franchise, *New Republic*, Oct. 31, 1964, at 17.

Is the Federal Government Helpless?, *New Republic*, Dec. 26, 1964, at 14.

Case of New York, *New Republic*, Dec. 26, 1964, at 11.

What Has Been Done Is Prologue: Carrying Out the Civil Rights Act, *New Republic*, Jan. 9, 1965, at 16.

Registering Negro Voters in the South, *New Republic*, Feb. 20, 1965, at 9.

Felix Frankfurter 1882–1965, *New Republic*, Mar. 6, 1965, at 7.

The Voting Rights Bill Is Tough, *New Republic*, Apr. 3, 1965, at 16.

Congress and the Poll Tax, *New Republic*, Apr. 24, 1965, at 11.

Amending the Voting Rights Bill, *New Republic*, May 1, 1965, at 10.

Speeding Up School Integration, *New Republic*, May 15, 1965, at 14.

Voting Rights Bill—Third Edition, *New Republic*, May 22, 1965, at 13.

Liberals and John Lindsay, *New Republic*, July 3, 1965, at 16.

House and Senate Voting Bills, *New Republic*, July 24, 1965, at 8.

Impeach Judge Cox, *New Republic*, Sept. 4, 1965, at 13.

Fighting Crime, *New Republic*, Sept. 18, 1965, at 11.

Homosexuality as Crime in North Carolina, *New Republic*, Dec. 12, 1965, at 5.

After the Arrest: Interrogation and the Right to Counsel, *New Republic*, Feb. 12, 1966, at 14.

Making the Best Use of the Police Force, *New Republic*, Mar. 12, 1966, at 8.

Forcing Desegregation through Title VI, *New Republic*, Apr. 9, 1966, at 8.

LBJ's Civil Rights Bill, *New Republic*, May 21, 1966, at 12.

Civil Rights' Dim Prospects, *New Republic*, Sept. 17, 1966, at 17.

Reexamining the Warren Report, *New Republic*, Jan. 7, 1967, at 25.

The Case for the Electoral College, *New Republic*, Jan. 28, 1967, at 15.

Law and Prudence in the Powell Case, *New Republic*, Feb. 25, 1967, at 9.

Antitrust Slowdown?, *New Republic*, May 20, 1967, at 15.

Obscenity Cases, *New Republic*, May 27, 1967, at 15.

Skelly Wright's Sweeping Decision, *New Republic*, July 8, 1967, at 11.

CBS and the Warren Report, *New Republic*, July 15, 1967, at 29.

Death Penalty Litigation, *New Republic*, Aug. 19, 1967, at 13.

Lawyers and More Lawyers, *New Republic*, Sept. 23, 1967, at 24.

Premature Verdict on Warren, *New Republic*, Oct. 7, 1967, at 36.

Return to Dallas, *New Republic*, Dec. 23, 1967, at 34.

Supreme Court: Internal Security Cases, *New Republic*, Jan. 6, 1968, at 21.

Frankfurter and Friend, *New Republic*, Feb. 3, 1968, at 27.

Spock-Coffin Case, *New Republic*, Mar. 2, 1968, at 23.

The Belated Civil Rights Legislation of 1968, *New Republic*, Mar. 30, 1968, at 11.

Senate Judiciary's Abominable Crime Bill, *New Republic*, May 25, 1968, at 13.

Crime, the Courts, and the Old Nixon, *New Republic*, June 15, 1968, at 8.

Back to the Attack, *New Republic*, June 22, 1968, at 28.

The Kennedy Cause, *New Republic*, July 20, 1968, at 42.

Fortas, Johnson, and the Senate, *New Republic*, Sept. 28, 1968, at 21.

Wait a Minute!, *New Republic*, May 10, 1969, at 11.

Mr. Justice Fortas, *New Republic*, May 17, 1969, at 9.

Close of the Warren Era, *New Republic*, July 12, 1969, at 13.

How to Beat Crime, *New Republic*, Aug. 30, 1969, at 10.

Student Demands and Academic Freedom, *New Republic*, Sept. 20, 1969, at 15.

Does It Stand Up?, *New Republic*, Nov. 1, 1969, at 13.

Desegregation: Where Do We Go from Here?, *New Republic*, Feb. 7, 1970, at 20.

The Debate over School Desegregation: A Reply, *New Republic*, Mar. 21, 1970, at 28.

The Tolerance of Violence on the Campus, *New Republic*, June 13, 1970, at 15.

The Revolution of Unreason, *New Republic*, Oct. 17, 1970, at 18.

Sharing Responsibility for War, *New Republic*, Sept. 25, 1971, at 15.

The Need for a War-Powers Bill, *New Republic*, Jan. 22, 1972, at 17.

What's Wrong with Nixon's Busing Bills?, *New Republic*, Apr. 22, 1972, at 19.

Powell's Day, *New Republic*, June 10, 1972, at 11.

Will the Democrats Survive Miami?, *New Republic*, July 15, 1972, at 17.

Untangling the Busing Snarl, *New Republic*, Sept. 23, 1972, at 21; Sept. 30, 1972, at 21.

More on Quotas, *New Republic*, Oct. 28, 1972, at 8.

The Overworked Court: A Reply to Arthur Goldberg, *New Republic*, Feb. 17, 1973, at 17.

Reconsideration: Edmund Burke, *New Republic*, Mar. 17, 1973, at 30.

The Tapes, Cox, Nixon, *New Republic*, Sept. 29, 1973, at 13.

What Now?, *New Republic*, Nov. 3, 1973, at 13.

Impeachment, *New Republic*, Nov. 10, 1973, at 9.

How Might Mr. Nixon Defend Himself?, *New Republic*, June 1, 1974, at 11.

Should Rodino Go to Court?, *New Republic*, June 8, 1974, at 11.

Articles in Other Publications

The Court: An Indictment Analyzed, *N.Y. Times Mag.*, Apr. 27, 1958, at 16.

Reapportionment and Liberal Myths, *Commentary*, June 1963, at 483; Nov. 1963, at 344.

Civil Rights Act of 1964, *Commentary*, Aug. 1964, at 33.

Much More Than Law Is Needed, *N.Y. Times Mag.*, Aug. 9, 1964, at 7.

Rosenberg Affair, *Commentary*, Jan. 1966, at 69; June 1966, at 20.

Is the Warren Court Too "Political"?, *N.Y. Times Mag.*, Sept. 25, 1966, at 30.

Failure of the Warren Report, *Commentary*, Oct. 1966, at 31; Apr. 1967, at 23.

Pornography and the Courts, *Commentary*, Nov. 1968, at 97.

Is Electoral Reform the Answer?, *Commentary*, Dec. 1968, at 41.

What is Happening to Morality Today?, *Yale Alumni Mag.*, Nov. 1969, at 53.

We've Shouted Down Our Sense of Balance, *Wash. Post*, June 14, 1970, at B2.

The Courts: The Need of Change, *N.Y. Times*, Oct. 22, 1970, at 47.

Judging the Chicago Trial, *Commentary*, Jan. 1971, at 31.

On Pornography: Concurring and Dissenting Opinions, *Public Interest*, Winter 1971, at 25 (with S. Kauffman, W. McWilliams & M. Cohen).

The Constitution and the War, *Commentary*, July 1972, at 49.

The "Uninhibited, Robust and Wide-Open" First Amendment: From *Sullivan* to the Pentagon Papers, *Commentary*, Nov. 1972, at 60.

Education in a Democracy: The Legal and Practical Aspects of School Busing, 3 *Human Rights* 53 (1973).

The Press and Government: Adversaries Without Absolutes, *Freedom at Issue*, May–June 1973, at 5.

Watergate and the Legal Order, *Commentary*, Jan. 1974, at 19.

Pornography, Censorship and Common Sense, *Reader's Digest*, Feb. 18, 1974, at 115 (interview).

On Mr. Jaworski's Quarrel with Mr. Nixon, *N. Y. Times*, May 23, 1974, at 41.

Book Reviews of:

The Legacy of Holmes and Brandeis by S. Konefsky (1956) and *The Brandeis Reader* by E. Pollack (1956), *30 New Eng. Q. 264* (1957).

Mr. Justice (A. Dunham & P. Kurland eds. 1956), *70 Harv. L. Rev. 1126* (1957).

Mr. Baruch by M. Coit (1957), *67 Yale L. J. 519* (1958).

The Supreme Court from Taft to Warren by A. Mason (1958), *12 J. Legal Ed. 287* (1959).

A Commentary on the Constitution of the United States by B. Schwartz (1963), *63 Colum. L. Rev. 1347* (1963).

Portrait of a Philosopher: Morris R. Cohen in Life and Letters by L. Rosenfield (1962), *56 Law Lib. J. 177* (1963).

Invitation to an Inquest by W. and M. Schneir (1965), *Commentary*, Jan. 1966, at 69.

The Death of a President by W. Manchester (1967), *New Haven Register*, Apr. 9, 1967, § 4, at 4.

Six Seconds in Dallas by J. Thompson (1967) and *Accessories After the Fact* by S. Meagher (1967), *New Republic*, Dec. 23, 1967, at 34.

Roosevelt and Frankfurter: Their Correspondence 1928–1945 (M. Freedman ed. 1967), *New Republic*, Feb. 3, 1968, at 27.

After the Assassination: A Positive Appraisal of the Warren Report by J. Sparrow (1967), *New Republic*, Mar. 23, 1968, at 41.

A Citizen's Dissent by M. Lane (1968), *New Republic*, June 22, 1968, at 28.

The End of Obscenity by Charles Rembar (1968), *Commentary*, Nov. 1968, at 97.

Justice: The Crisis of Law, Order and Freedom in America by R. Harris (1970), *New Republic*, Apr. 18, 1970, at 21.

Justice Joseph Story and the Rise of the Supreme Court by G. Dunne (1971), *N. Y. Times Book Rev.*, May 30, 1971, at 3.

Index